WOLOVE

A HAITIAN-AMERICAN'S DREAM

Thanks Ms Pat Rodriguez,
For thinkink about
helping us with our
project in Haiti!

Paul

BERTONY PAUL

© 2013 Bertony Paul

ISBN-13: 978-1494303990
ISBN-10: 149430399X
US Copyright Number: 1-1034996351

Author's Picture by Michael Nkwantabisa
Cover Design by Nhyira

THE AMERICAN TRIANGLE OF SUCCESS

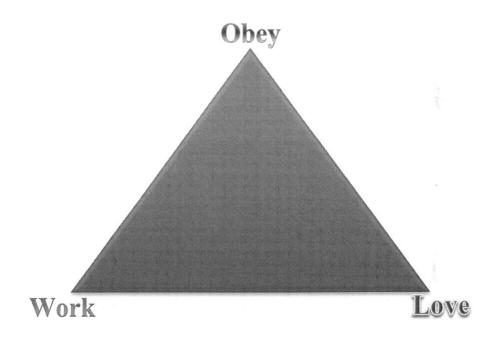

DEDICATION

After eating a dream salad –
Thinking, dying,
Losing everything
Learning something –
I want to thank my Salsa family
Yajaira, Sara, Martina, Mario, John James and
Barbara.

Also, Lizeth, Jean Louis, Roy, Helena, Kida, and
Jennifer.

Especially, my Salsa teacher, Vanessa Beltrán-
Medina for keeping me dancing.

Finally, I thank Kaden Paul
For loving me

AUTHOR'S WORD

I have longed to collaborate with morally or
socially progressive people in sharing the ideas
encapsulated in Wolove: *the American Triangle of
Success*. I have looked forward to implement these
ideas with citizens and students in Haiti and the
Americas. After publishing Wolove: *a Haitian-
American Dream* (in Creole and English), I think it
is time. We must work together for the emergence
of a new group of citizens who are united in
purpose and thrive to become stronger, in socio-
economic terms.

TABLE OF CONTENTS

Chapter   **Page**

PREFACE

In Creole, we say, *someone else will never take care of you. You must take care of yourself.* This expression has become integrated in our hearts and minds. It is part of our way of life in the Haitian community. Today, we are at the cusp of ending this situation of sitting and waiting for opportunities to drop on our laps. We have to take charge and be responsible for the end of situations that control us and makes us miserable. At this extraordinary moment in our lives, we should ask ourselves the fundamental question, *what can I do for myself?* While you are reading this book, ask yourself, *what are the solutions to our problems?*

When we knock at the door of a respected person, we inquire, *are you available?* The author of this book, Bertony Paul, is a wonderful Haitian. He is from Verrettes, Haiti. From the time he was a little boy, Bertony saw how his parents worked hard every day to bring about change in their community. In the same way, when he became an adult, he decided to continue the work his parents had started. Paul went to church to learn a better way of life. He learned how to forgive and be humble. He traveled to Montpellier, France where he was introduced to theology. This was something very important in his life because that gave him wisdom. It gave him access to profound knowledge.

Bertony always says: "When I am working, I see God in everyone." Upon returning to Haiti in 1997, he began teaching spoken French at the National School of Arts where he wrote *A Vous l'Amour en Parole* (For You, My Love in Words), which he will publish it next year. One of his students took part in a Christmas singing contest and won second place. His burning desire was to start working on change in his country. Later on, he took a job with the government where he was posted in the North western part of Haiti.

His job was to teach people how to change their entire way of life, in order to increase productivity. The government asked him to organize the people to work their farms and accomplish multiple tasks. Unfortunately, things ended in disappointment. This broke Bertony's heart. The training was focused on fertilizer, seed and tool distribution. It did not tackle the root causes of the farmers' inability to break the cycle of poverty. Bottom line, the training was designed to keep the government, at that time, to stay in power. Bertony resigned from his post but he did not give up. He continued to work with his people. He did not want politics to get in the way of productivity. He moved to another country to continue to work, in other ways, for a change in Haiti.

In 2002, Bertony came to the United States of America. He worked long shifts daily and met people from different cultural backgrounds. This helped him immensely to build a new way of thinking, in a quest to solve some of Haiti's endemic problems. The idea of *WOLOVE* describes what we can and must do to change our lives. We can become proactive citizens and stop waiting for others to do everything for us. We must act if we want to join the developed world and make poverty a thing of the past. This is a blueprint for the reconstruction of Haiti.

In *Wolove*, Bertony underlines the importance of all that that we can do for a better life and prosperity. He demonstrates how we should work smarter for the future of our children and our country. Waiting for chances to appear out of thin air does not get anything changed. The idea of *Wolove* suggests that we illuminate our consciousness with information necessary to the attainment of change. The author entreats us to give ourselves a choice of developing a better trajectory for our lives. With history and current affairs, he describes how to think differently, how to work together and how to act in sync for change. With the *Wolove* project, we will learn how to combat the despondency that has paralyzed life in Haiti. The primary objective for *Wolove* is to create hope for the people of Haiti.

Bertony believes in hard work and knows very well that that is the spine of development for all people. He also believes in the wisdom in obeying the law. We all know that if we live within the confines of law, we will take positive steps forward. If there are no rules in place and everyone does what they like, we will go nowhere. Finally, the love we have for our country Haiti will not allow us to stand aside and watch her falter and fail. When we love our country, we treasure everything it has. We will do everything we can to make it look beautiful. We must come together to make our country work towards its best interests.

The *Wolove* project is a new approach in utilizing the abilities and acumen of the Haitian people. We must open our eyes to see another possible vision for Haiti. This new dream will establish a reality stable enough to continue for many generations. The costs that the earthquake's aftershocks brought on us cannot stop us from carving a prosperity that we deserve. Let us live a new life with the principles that *Wolove* suggests. If we commit to these principles and see them through, Haiti will regain the status of *The Pearl of the Antilles*. We can attain the economic freedom that has eluded us for so long.

D. Beauplan

LAYING A FOUNDATION OF WORDS

At a time when cholera has devoured strength from the small body of Haiti, the country needs jolts of hope and possibility.

This time, the objective is not to put the country to sleep, but to shake the heck out of the Haitian people. It is time to wash the county of the unhelpful things that have latched themselves to our national psyche through these years. We must begin to put in efforts towards progress on the paths we have chosen to pursue. This is because we have discovered education as a viable means to achieve economic revolution. A new Haiti shall emerge where rich and poor people work together. The rich can become richer and the poor can become rich too, by investing in tourism and other small businesses. The nation of Haiti stands to benefit from the situation where responsibility and proactivity continuously create opportunity.

From the 1950s to the 1970s, Haiti was the number one country tourist destination in the Caribbean area. It was in Haiti that Hilary and Bill Clinton had their honeymoon. Without fail, we need to work hard, obey the laws and love our country. This creates conducive environments for tourists to visit. These are integral steps toward an end to the cycle of poverty. I do not understand why most of us only talk about national pride and have chosen to forget those who fought for us. It is our sacrosanct duty to continue what they started. This means that Haiti needs help and should accept the support of any country, especially the U.S.A. This is because Haitian made sacrifices in the bloody war of 1779 against the British in Savannah, Georgia. Haiti played an important role in the birth of the American dream. That is why we have decided to plant a sample of the American dream in every corner of Haiti. This is in support of the creation of a new Haitian dream, with and for the Haitian people. We need to stop fighting and take a stake in Haiti's future. If we cannot do this simple task, we will all die and nobody will care. Let us learn to live together, love life and appreciate beauty. Let us spend not waste time on demonstrations, devastation and corruption. Let us invest more time in working, in motivating ourselves and in conserving our natural resources. We have to create awareness about what needs to be done. Communication, harmonization and socialization will open new doors for our nation. Volunteer to work with our government and friends of Haiti to bring peace to the country. Let us keep our neighborhoods clean and opt for renewable energy. In partnership with various counties (using *Wolove* principles), we will develop small hotel resorts for tourists. Patriotism will save Haiti if we work hard at what matters. Haitians have to learn how to make tires, instead of burning them on the streets. Liberation comes from within. It is only complete when it changes what is outside. As long as responsibility is a priority, there is nothing that can derail a dream. Work shall save Haiti. Obedience to the law shall save Haiti. Love shall save Haiti.

Bertony Paul

WOLOVE

Moun ki bezwen deyò, chache chemen pòt.
He who must go out, searches for the door.
(Haitian Proverb)

Haiti has prompted centuries since she was in an obscure relationship with the darkness. What is more, nobody cares. When Haiti looks around, there is no help coming from anywhere. All her allies and friends have abandoned her. Those countries she had helped in the past are reluctant to come to her aid. Haiti is like a woman who is looking at her watch, wondering when *Sendenden*, her lover from *ziltik* (Haitian word for faraway) will come and save her. Haiti is this beautiful girl they used to call *La Perle des Antilles* or *Haiti Cherie* a long, long time ago. I long to see her beauty restored. I long to see her smile again.

What does Wolove means?

Wolove is a spiritual triangle with 3 equal sides and with three signs (WO♥) which have brought a lot of success in those countries where they practice them. But, each sign means something in English. You can learn English for free if you go on YouTube and search for *iFriendnet Organization* to see the lessons.

Wolove simply means

W = Work Hard

O = Obey the Laws

♥ = Love your country

Work, obey and love. This is the summary of a well-lived life. This is the diagnosis of a life going places. There is no substitute for these three things. Anyone (or community) who neglects them, does so at their own peril. As an immigrant, I have observed many things that make America great. Imperfect as it is, it thrives on basic principles that have stood the test of time. Critical among those principles are work, obedience and love. I have personally seen American society thrive on these cardinal principles. These are the same principles that form what I have coined, The American Triangle of Success. Applied at personal, communal and national levels, these principles have not failed to yield results over and over again. This book is about how Haitians can learn, and inculcate, the core values of American community. This is also a reminder to Americans to continue what has made their nation great throughout these years. It is important to revisit these principles, from time to time, and to place them on the pedestal of our collective attention. This is to ensure that retrogression does not occur neither in this present generation nor the ones to come. Much more than history books have led us to believe, Haiti has played a far more pivotal role in the forming (and framing) of Continental America's socio-political landscape. It is time for the great nation of Haiti to borrow a few pointers from the equally great nation of the United States. This is

Sometimes, when we see our brothers and sisters get out of work, they look like zombies. The situation is hard, together with the heat and those big snakes in Florida. They wear heavy clothing, hats and gloves to protect themselves. They never complain. They reckon that they are not here for vacation. They are here because they want a better life. Here, in the United States of America, you cannot sit down and wait for a Western Union or MoneyGram transfer from nobody. If you want something, you do what must be done right to get it.

After a few years, when they have enough savings, these Haitian immigrants build houses back home in Haiti. They purchase homes in the United States and send their children to college. This is why Haitians are number two in the black demographic, in terms of diplomas and net worth. They have exceeded all expectations. This should be a source of national pride. These folks deserve congratulations and appreciation for the sacrifices they continually make for their children and to Haiti. They always send help home. Our Haitian brethren in diaspora fully recognize the essence of sacrifice in the quest for success. Where there is no pain, there is no gain. The pursuit of happiness goes through terrains of difficulty. We must inculcate the love of work, compliance with the law and togetherness into our group consciousness, if we are intent on seeing change. Sacrifice is critical to success. We must endeavor to live accordingly to the priorities that are critical to the attainment of social prosperity in Haiti. One of the cardinal requirements of success is that one must not be averse to work. Not just any work but work that has compound effect. Work that changes destinies of individuals and their families. Work that builds communities. Work that improves the state of nations.

What we learn from this example that if the Haitians can do this overseas, there is any reason why they cannot be successful in their own country. The people who see in themselves the answers to their problems are the people most easy to help. Every problem is pregnant with its own solutions. Our brethren in the United States exceeded our expectations, not because of luck, but because of their willingness to work, obey and love their communities. There are three things in life with guaranteed results: work, obedience and love. This is what *Wolove* is all about. So, let us get to work.

2- **Roselande Accilien**

Don't wait for extraordinary opportunities. Seize common occasions and make them great. Weak men wait for opportunities; strong men make them.

- Orison Swett Marden (author of *He Who Thinks He Can*)

Here is the story of Roselande Accilien, a wonderful Haitian woman. Ms. Roselande is a small business woman, a light that shines in the Haitian darkness. As we all know, most girls love playing with dolls. But for Roselande, it was a totally different story. At a very young age, she started playing with money. She started learning business skills, putting the lunch money her mother gave her together with that of her classmates to form a fund she could borrow more from. When Roselande had enough money, she bought a bag of candy and started her first small business. Fast forward from that candy bag and today, Ms. Roselande owns a cosmetics store in Cap Haitian, the second largest city in Haiti. The whole country should know about this inspiring story, a living proof that there can be a change in the Haitian mentality of waiting and praying for opportunities. We urge the people of Cap Haitian to take their kids and go shopping at Roselande's store on Rue 7J # 109, Cap Haitian. That woman is amazing. She keeps all the prices of the goods in her head. We intend to lift Ms. Roselande up as a role model for Haitians to emulate. Her indefatigable drive is critical to her success. She did not allow excuses of existence to lull her into the stupor of inactivity. This woman proves, over and over again, that the power of perseverance can change the most difficult f circumstances. The starting point is to find what works and to stick to it, come what may. We, on our part at ifriendnett.org, would like to join with some interested business people in the US who can help develop and computerize small businesses like Ms. Roselande's. Finally, we say small businesses are struggling everywhere and more than 90% of them do not make it past their second year. Roselande was lucky and started taking care of herself at the age of 14, whereas most Haitians, from birth until they die, never have a job. It is their parents, in Haiti or abroad, who have to take care of them. This is a behavior that can be challenged and changed. This is why we are sharing Roselande's history to the rest of the country.

Roselande's story needs to be told. It is one of the many success stories happening in Haiti. This is one story that must be recounted to every interested Haitian. Therefore, if we learn small business skills at an early age, we are more likely to become productive and responsible citizens. We have been acclimatized to futility and that must change. We have to recalibrate our thinking and push ourselves to the places we seek to be. Success is the sum of consistent acts done in the spirit of change that benefits all. It stems out of a relentless challenge to the status quo. Roselande is a living example whose trajectory in life can be emulated, in the best interest of our children and benefit of Haiti.

3- **Bill Gates**

Whatever you do, do it with all your might. Work at it, early and late, in season and out of season, not leaving a stone unturned, and never deferring for a single hour that which can be done just as well now.
- P. T Barnum

Bill Gates is one of the richest men in the world. Well, if you do not know his name, you are already using electronic systems that he created. If you touch a computer, this is a result of Bill Gates' innovation. If you have a cell phone, you are using elements of his invention as well.

This guy did not finish his studies. He wanted to create a revolutionary business through technology. He began working with a company that built computers in the 70s. That company was

IBM. But during all this time, Gates was planning to go further in his career and become rich. He set out to achieve his dream by visiting another society where people worked very hard in the area of technology. Bill spent time there to learn their secrets until one day he knew exactly what to do.

After his finding, Bill did not go somewhere to celebrate. He went straight to work. He slept in his offices and never took a vacation until he made a program called Microsoft. Microsoft is not a computer, but you need it to make a computer work. You need it if you want to go online or you want to write or make a word processor.

This program is so well done that almost all computers that you purchase have a component of Microsoft. Anyone who laughed because he humbled himself to learn what they know now stays quiet before the success of this man.

After he stopped working directly in informatics, Gates decided to do volunteer work. He opened clinics in parts of the world to help people in need. He fuses this with his technology because he knows that is the most instrumental thing we need in this 21st century.

The most admirable thing we can glean from this story is that, when you want to do something, do not be afraid to be disappointed, nor fear of learning from others. That is how you get to know what you need. If you do not learn how to swim, it will be impossible to get out from the sea of misery that is drowning

Haiti. Let us start learning a new Haiti, with Wolove and iFriendnett.org, today. A life of dedicated work, devotion to ethics and a disposition towards the good of people is the platform for success. We can get all the education and riches in the world but if we neglect the essence of work, we fail ourselves. If we tolerate disrespect for the law and nonchalance as our attitude towards our neighbors, we derail our own dreams.

In April 2013, Socrate Paul founded with me the first Wolove association in Haiti called Wolove Saint Raphael Association. It was a step in the right direction because it capitalized on the willingness of the community to do anything possible to bring about change. We have to step up to the plate when it comes to things that affect us directly. It is time to take the driver seat of our individual and collective destinies. Nobody will do it for us.

In his article, *7 Secrets of Success*, Andrew McChesney listed the following attitudes as the foundations of success. The attitude of respecting people, no matter their status. The attitude of proper time management. The attitude of honoring promises. The attitude of perpetual learning. The attitude of humility. The attitude of leadership by example and that of love. McChesney listed these attitudes as the secrets of Russian billionaires. This begs the question: if individuals can make themselves successful through these simple principles, why can't nations do the same? It is time for us to look at ourselves in the mirror and do something about what we see. An end should be put to this morbid tolerance of misery. We have to come up with ways to save our dear nation from the pits of poverty and adversity. Other nations have pulled themselves out of dire conditions and have become success stories. Their stories became possible only when the people shook themselves out of the shame and stupor to say, enough is enough.

There are many examples of individuals, communities and nations who found ideas that worked for them and followed them through. The world will not hand over free lunches to us. We must work hard for everything that comes our way. It is not luck that opens the way to freedom. It is labor towards an excellent end. Haiti now stands at the cusp of its socio-economic liberation, partly due to the proliferation of technology as one of the instruments of development. We must jump on to the bandwagon of knowledge seekers and get all the expertise we need to apply to our circumstances. Our people need knowledge to advance our society. We will let ourselves down if we drop the ball in finding solutions that lay right before our very eyes.

WORKING HARD IS A SACRED DUTY

Chita pa bay.
Sitting doesn't give.
(Haitian Proverb)

Our circumstances are difficult but we can make them easier to bear when we come together as a unit to find common ground. We can work towards our mutual progress. The willingness to work, as an intrinsic value, is an aegis against poverty. Hard work does not break bones but it sure breaks the back of poverty. Work is good for the individual and his/her community. Through work, we state to our communities how much we are willing to exert ourselves to keep things going. Let us join together and build the courage to work hard, day and night, for 12 to 16 hours a day, on the road of life. More often than not, our Haitian small farmers work on their land only when it rains. Then they settle down and wait for next year's rain. Even though in the rainy season, they work hard, they do not produce enough to live on. To survive, they leave the countryside to find work in the cities where they live in conditions far worse than those back home. But in countries where people work their farms with a plan in mind, time is not wasted. Those farmers produce more than what they eat. This is what makes exports possible.

I remember what happened in Montagneux, a small village in south France. Jacques, a French peasant, who lived in this mountainous area, was a hard worker. This peasant worked 15 hours a day on his farm. He did not rest. He worked all the time. Even when it snowed or during the hot summers, he worked inside a special house called *serre*. To till the soil, he used a small machine in which he changed heads for each job he is doing. I must also state that he got a loan from the bank to purchase all the equipment he needed on his farm. There are no bank loans for the Haitian peasant farmers. However, we must not lose hope because we can have everything we want if we sit down with our authorities to find solutions. We must educate ourselves to be problem-solvers. I use Jacque's example to illustrate how hardworking individuals, in collaboration with a supportive banking system, can determine the trajectory of their lives.

We need to work with our elected officials in love and respect. That does not also mean that we sit and wait for them to bring us everything. We can organize ourselves to create small credit facilities in our communities. Small business skills training can be provided, together with the introduction of modern agricultural techniques. In the meantime, we need to work closely with our authorities and other foreign friends who want to help but not to profiteer from our poverty. A French peasant volunteer, trained in agronomy, spent time working in Vyekay, Haiti with small farmers in the Saint Dominique community. His name was Jacques. He was a hard working individual who tapped water 24/7 after designing a system specifically watered the seed. In the end, this well-educated Frenchman serves as a great example for us. He is the very epitome of skill and sacrifice. We do not have to be trained in agronomy, in order to cultivate our land. The path to change our lives is long, but we cannot give up. In Haiti, we don't use GPS to go anywhere. We ask for directions and never get lost. This shows that if we are committed enough to seek help to educate ourselves on how to bring water everywhere, we can do it. Together, we can make Haiti a better place for everyone.

One of the educators on iFriendnett.org (Lenji Jacob) was using Skype to teach English to a group of Haitian students in the Dominican Republic. During one training session, he asked the students: "what can poor people do to change their lives?" And they all answered, "Pray to God or wait for the rich to help." The teacher responded by saying, 'as we gather to pray or learn English, we can join together to change our lives too. The rich people, they get together under a strong intellectual support to become rich. They do not wait for anybody to help them. Alternatively, I can tell you, if you take a small stick from the tree, any of us can break it but if we put 40 sticks together neither one of us can break them all together. And as well as if we all join together to practice *Wolove*, there is nobody on the face of the earth that can stop us from becoming rich and stay rich.' A stop must be put to the practice of waiting for assistance. Haiti needs to set up systems that provide assistance, even in basic forms, to those who need it. Continuance of the practice of reaching for handouts must cease. The time has come to produce and provide for ourselves.

Thereafter, Lenji told the students another story. He said that "there was a mother with 5 children, she gave each of them $ 500 and said, "go out for a month, do whatever you like with the money and, you only need to provide me a report at the end."

After a month, they all returned home.

The first child said: "I bought clothes and food. I also partied with the rest of the money. I don't a penny left."

The second said: "I put my money in the bank. I didn't spend it. It's still there. The only thing is that the bank takes $5 a month, for maintenance."

The third said: "I bought an item at a discount. After I resold it, I made $500 in profits."

The fourth said: "I pooled my money with that of three other people. We invested the sum. Each of us had a profit of $2000."

The last one said: 'I divided the money into 20 parts, investing them in 20 small Wolove businesses. I made $5,000 for the month.'"

We hope you continue to think ways to change our lives and develop Haiti.

In the USA, most of the jobs are from 26 million small businesses. This is a good and successful economic model for all those countries who want a better life. To succeed economically today, you do not have to reinvent the wheel. You only need to replicate successful models like the Grameen Bank (banking for the poor) in Bangladesh, which started investing a few dollars in 1976. Fast forward, for more than 2 years, Grameen Bank is lending money to the people of New York. Let us join together with government officials and friends of Haiti to create many small businesses with access to banks where we can borrow and pay on time. Funding is integral to the realization of dreams. The great thing is that we do not need a million dollars to begin a million dollar dream. Little by little, step by step, a dream on course will find means to translate itself into reality. All that needs to be done is to start and not stall in our efforts. It is through our efforts and the results we get that we attract interest. Inactivity has no magnetic powers on money. Wealth likes to associate itself with work well done in communities with promise. We can properly implement these ideas of collaboration in our communities. There are many individuals, communities and nations who are willing to help us. However, we must differentiate ourselves by working hard on the foundations of prosperity so that we will not become burdens on those who decide to help us. There is an African proverb that goes: *The community pushes upward the man who climbs a strong tree.* We must climb the strong trees of work and industry. We must steer the wheels of community towards prosperity. Our communities must encourage innovation and ingenuity. We must identify youth with promise and provide them with the support they need to be of use to Haiti. As long as we are willing to do what it takes to introduce change in our way of doing things, there will be no cap to our potential as a nation. Bottom line, we work hard not to chase after wealth but to attract it.

1 - Discipline

You must be professional under all circumstances, under any regime.

-   Vladimir Vilde (Russian multimillionaire)

One definition of discipline is *to punish someone for a moral infraction*. Another definition, which is being used in this book, is the willingness to do things differently and consistently to achieve the best of results. The reason why discipline takes longer, as a practice, is that it depends primarily on self-control. People are averse to discipline because it connotes being controlled. People hate being controlled. However, with discipline, the person doing the control is you. You set goals for yourself and you hold yourself to standards that push you towards excellence. You exist in a realm of accountability and probity to yourself. That should not be a bad thing per se. That actually sounds like freedom. But let us not digress. The hard truth is that nothing worthy can be attained and maintained without discipline. To become better, we must find a way to end our tolerance of the usual. Life, whether it treats us well or not, depends on discipline. This is because without discipline, everything else is lost.

Discipline, as in the second definition, is what concerns us in these efforts towards the building of a better Haiti. Subsequently, when we talk about discipline, we assume it in the essence of a rigid social structure that takes us through a system of thought. This structure, when followed through, productively brightens our consciousness of knowledge. Consequently, we must work together to create a new social dream for Haiti that is higher than all the individual ones. Let us think of partnerships that enable us to create and implement new ideas.

Today let us give ourselves a tool of thought that we shall swear 77 times 7 times:

We will never say or do anything that does not promote the interest and prosperity of the Haitian society.

Surely we think through everything we do in life before we actually do them. Before we eat, we think about food. Before we go to work, we think about work. We see clearly that it is our thoughts that guide us. Let us organize our thoughts and create what we need, in order to build a solid foundation for Haiti. The best way to invigorate one's mind is to be part of a society where there is a national plan of education for all members of that society. Even though education comes in varied forms, its goal is the individual development of each citizen. Where each citizen is enlightened, the community reaches a critical mass of thought that translates into action for the good of all. This means that we are lucky together and unlucky apart. Individually, we must contemplate upon and complete the things that take us towards socio-economic prosperity. Collectively, we must brainstorm (and implement) the various options that lie before us. A well thought idea does not exist in fear of failure. It thrives in the actions of the people who molded it. It will be helpful if we devote ourselves to the good of whatever we do as a collective. By doing so, our minds are set free to find solutions that lie in plain sight. A proper mindset is essential to the work at hand. We must continue to train our minds to find ways to establish material, intellectual and cultural development in our country. Our mental faculties exist as tools in discovering and using the many intricacies of existence to our advantage.

How do we understand the word *development*? As with human beings, words are born. They grow and die out of obscurity. Haiti is under construction today. The word *development* is the spice in everyone's sauce. To acquaint ourselves with development in Haiti today, we give up on the *sitting and waiting* way of life. Development begins in the mind and ends in action. It requires discipline and a willingness to sacrifice. Development in the Haitian society today means approaching old problems with new approaches. It means we have to find optimal results in everything we do. We have to produce more than what we need so we can export what remains to other countries. For instance, if you decide to grow sweet potatoes for only the Haitian people, you are not developing anything. You are only drifting from season to season, hoping to survive each one of them. That is not the new Haitian dream. We need to work smart together because we have the duty to ensure that we feed ourselves and others. It is imperative for us to learn and use modern techniques as means to work our farms. Efficient farming requires less labor and yields more results. This was a small example. In every domain of industry, we have to increase the production capacity. We have opportunities in culture, technology, goods and services. We must do work on these priorities around the clock.

Finally, discipline is something that we must apply in everyday life. A community that is disciplined prepares everything in advance. What is more; we prepare the day, week and month and year. In his article, *The Power of Good Habits*, David Lee lists the following abilities as integral to success: the ability to develop a schedule, the ability to do things ahead of time, the ability to be confident in one's trajectory and the ability to separate needs from wants. Let us make realistic projections, based on present circumstances, and work hard to exceed them. As we have no control of Mother Nature, discipline helps to weather the many surprises of life. We must be in the habit of imagining better communities and giving those dreams a chance to live. A popular American axiom goes, *if you fail to plan, you plan to fail*. If we do nothing, *nothing* will do us in.

We must discipline ourselves to desire excellence and pursue it with all our heart. Until we develop this, we will waste our efforts for nothing. I heard a saying that inspired me throughout these years. It says, through discipline, you find your freedom. I concurred with that saying the very first time I heard it. Haitians can become free from socio-economic hardships if we subject ourselves to discipline. We cannot have a happy-go-lucky approach to things that matter and expect them to bloom at sunrise. Such wishful thinking must be purged from our collective mindset. If we want prosperity badly, we must work for it. It will not come through handouts and loans. It will not come through corruption and nepotism. It will only come when we quit feeding our excuses and clean up our act as a people.

2 - Bring prosperity to our families.

In my work in Haiti, I've seen the hugely positive effects that happen when people come together to build something in the middle of the most desperate situations.
- Olivia Wilde

If each Haitian can commit to being a source of prosperity to his/her community, imagine how our communities would bloom? Prosperity does not come out of the blues. It comes as a reward for good planning and meticulous work. It comes after discipline has been put into effort and excellence has been raised as the standard for any kind of business. Every Haitian, educated or not, is capable of greatness. The challenge is how to break the cycle of being lackadaisical and lax to opportunities that lay around us. We must put our efforts into the little work we find and help it expand into something that provides a livelihood for more people. No one has monopoly over prosperity. However, it is attracted to an iron will that works its way to excellence.

Hardworking individuals are blessings to their communities, who in turn are blessings to the nation. Where many people are working or when there are many jobs, we term that place as a prosperous society. In Haiti, where there are no jobs, we can speak of a society of misère because there is no peace of mind. There will be no jobs where everyone is sitting and waiting for opportunity. Jobs are not from heaven. They come from women and men who work hard, obey laws and love their country. In all honesty, to reach prosperity in Haiti, each of us should help ourselves. If every Haitian continues to swim out alone in that tumultuous sea of poverty, we all will drown. We will never reach anywhere. Because if we do not join together to swim together, we will all perish together. Skill will never be in short supply but prosperity (or not) depends on whether we are nonchalant about work (or not). How can we fare in a difficult world if we find the call to work a difficult one? Hard work is not only the use of muscles in excruciating tasks. It also means the use of the mind to find effective ways of leveraging existing skill for more results. There is no excuse to refrain from work. It is a basic requirement of existence.

In Haiti, the prime objective is to create opportunities. Those opportunities create jobs. Those jobs bring in prosperity. Prosperity is a result. It is not random. The community that works hard against its problems is a community that prospers. How can we generate more jobs and bring prosperity to Haiti? One of the first things that would be possible is to transform our dirty and informal businesses into clean and formal small businesses. Our thriving business should have access to small credit so they can expand and hire more people. We need more thorough leadership to function as initiatives bring affluence to Haiti. On behalf of the Haitian people, government should borrow money (or partner with private capital) to create artificial lakes and water pipes leading into the mountains. This will help farmers to create small businesses in all ranges of production which, in turn, will bring more abundance to Haiti. We must collaborate with sister nations to create international marketplaces for products made in Haiti. It baffles me when young girls and boys, after they finish high school, think that they no longer belong to the farm. If Maurice Sixto, one of our great comedians were to be alive, he would have joked at their expense, by saying in Haitian: "bali boulva!"

We are all learning many ways to make Haiti great again. No idea is a waste of time, as long as it keeps us in the right direction towards development. What we think of ourselves is more important than what others think of us. Why is it that the populations of Baptiste, Gros Morne and Jacmel are not looking to partner with investors to produce more coffee? Why are they not willing to transform it into a finished product ready for local and international consumption? If we do not change our attitudes towards development, we will see profits from the sale of coffee trickle into hands of foreign investors and not into Haiti's hands.

May we all have jobs. May everyone eat well. Let us be happy in the hope that Haiti may have peace and be a place where body and mind are in harmony. We seek a nation secured for all and comfortable for those willing to do the work.

3 - Make big dreams and work hard to achieve them.

Cherish your visions and your dreams as they are children of your soul, the blueprints of your ultimate achievements.
- Napoleon Hill

A friend once told me that if our dreams are not big enough to scare us, then they are not big enough to change the world. I think he was right. One of the things that can save Haiti is a collection of big dreams. Poverty has made it normal to dream very little dreams but change can only come if our dreams have enough not just to save Haiti but the world as well. We must encourage our citizens to write their dreams down and plan on how to actualize them in phases. There is no big dream that started big. A big dream has to start out small to test its objectives. Dreams that have changed the world have gone through a lot of realistic revisions. However, the core ideals have always remained. Haiti needs to become a nation of dreamers and doers. It is okay to dream but we must follow through with action. There is no obstacle too great, no excuse too paramount. If flowers can grow in concrete, dreams can flourish in Haiti.

Poverty affects all races. No country holds monopoly on poverty or prosperity. Our progress or retrogress depends solely on our actions. The Haitian people made history. We are world class citizens who do wonders. Nevertheless, we are still poor. We are still begging for money, food and clothes. But, what we really need is applicable knowledge that forms the basis of socioeconomic development in advanced countries. Haiti must make a choice to lock all doors of the laboratories of poverty and throw the key into the sea. It should open its doors to many research centers to create job opportunities.

All great societies rely on knowledge and know its importance. They create research centers or laboratories to brainstorm and find solutions for all types of problems. This social posture makes them ready to solve new problems that may arise in the future. To get out of poverty and to secure a better future, we must begin to work identifying the roots of our problems. We have to create series of laboratory research with collaboration between public and private sector together with the rest of society. Here is an example that can help us understand how working together can help keep us out of poverty and lead us to progress. In the early 2000s, I worked for PDID (Integrated Development Project Desarmes) under the direction of Reverent Frantz Grandroit. In the fifth section, Dophine in Verrettes county (which was one of the project intervention areas), I had the chance to work with two groups of peasants (top and bottom Dofine) who were living like dogs and cats. This means that the patties did not care about each other. They always had many conflicts. I was happy to serve as a negotiator between the two groups. They had to work together to capture and bring water to the top of a mountain to farm all year long. I assisted the two groups to create 15 small forests to learn planting trees and 15 small fish ponds to get protein. I wish people of Dophine will continue to progress together to change their lives and country.

In every city and village you see the same message: 50, 15 and 10 gourdes. For those who do not understand, this is the amount of money you get paid for winning first second and third places, respectively, when you play lotto for one gourdes (Haitian currency). Most people who play lotto do so because they have a dream. The chicken fighters also bring their roosters to the arena because they have dreams. Through both cases, we realize that the Haitian people are full of dreams but we want to create dreams while we are wide awake. We are talking about dreams for a country that cannot sleep. Haiti cannot sleep even though most Haitians are still in pajamas. Thus, we will want to talk about a dream with our eyes wide-awake, where we all dreamed about gels together. We want a prosperous Haiti in 20, 30 or 50 years. It is up to us to educate ourselves and to find ways to realize our dreams. I remember the 70s-80s era, the city Port-au-Prince never sleep even I do not remember what they used to do. However, the new Haiti that we want to invent each and every day together we hope that Haiti will never have to go to sleep. All Haiti will be dynamic and will work 24/7 for our dreams to become reality.

The excuse of bad circumstances does not hold at the court of perseverance. We cannot allow tough conditions to tear our dreams apart. We must fight to keep our dreams alive. The many systems we have permitted that have produced a steady line of poverty and failure must be abolished. We must enter the critical phase of our national odyssey where we cut off everything that has not worked for us. The grand irony in all this is that most developing countries have vast reserves of resources that should place them in more developed states. However, the problem lies in the management of priorities. We cannot tolerate mediocrity if we desire prosperity. We cannot reward corruption if we want progress. Bad habits have to die for good ones to thrive. We can usher in an era of socio-economic progress by purging the clogs of ineptitude. Bottom line, we bear responsibility for what happens to us.

4 - In our backyard, we have to grow fruits and vegetables to eat and put the rest out to sell.

Nothing can bring you peace but yourself. Nothing can bring you peace but the triumph of principles.
  - Ralph Waldo Emerson (Self-Reliance)

Building on the previous idea, I want to state how important it is to grow one's food. In America, a lot of people do not grow what they eat so they have no way of checking what was used on the crops. In Haiti, we are blessed to be able to grown fruits and vegetables in our backyards. We must enhance that habit to a wide scale effort where every household grows more than it needs. This will result in an abundance that can be exported or bought by government to establish a food bank. It is essential that we think big in all that we do, especially in areas that are already yielding results for us. I can only imagine how such a practice will drastically cut down the food needs of our nation. We hold, in our hands, the keys to our freedom and we must put our heads together to make these things happen. Our society has to open itself to the possibilities that exist right under our feet. The land has to be utilized in every way possible. We must derive maximum benefit from the wealth hidden in our soils. Haiti is surrounded by countless opportunities but we have trained our eyes to see only the obstacles. Our perceptions have to change. We have to retrain ourselves to see opportunities.

In Haiti, we have wild dogs that come after you if you do not have a stick to protect yourself. It is not a secret to anyone that Haitian peasants live in a space that we call lakou (yard) more often than not. They have their houses and still have a small garden on the side. We come to ask you all to improve on this widespread practice to help curb hunger and to help you generate extra pocket money. In each village, we should have discussions about development fields. These are fields in which a rotation of crops is grown year-round. This can be done in collaboration with local authorities and foreign friends who can help us move forward in our research to develop such fields. This ensures that we will never have any shortages in production of fruits and vegetables at any period of the year.

As a nation, we must begin to accommodate new and vibrant ideas. The nation has to develop a social repository of ideas where each individual can access and utilize. Haiti cannot plan for just today and tomorrow. We cannot plan for just ourselves. We must involve our neighbors in this venture to guarantee our success. Progress is something that requires active commitment and action from people. Wishing for a good society is an exercise in futility. We must work for it. In essence, people have to be given tools to work out their future. It is essential for people to understand how important it is for them to be in charge of where their communities are headed. Our dreams must be backed by fierce determination. They cannot exist on their own, especially in circumstances such as ours. It is, therefore, our sacred responsibility to attain every resource necessary to our rejuvenation as a people. The price of such resurgence is the willingness to learn what is possible and act on it.

5 - As rain falls, put many seeds in the soil.

It's always about timing. If it's too soon, no one understands. If it's too late, everyone's forgotten.
 -   Anna Wintour

Land must produce when rain falls. Let us channel water everywhere and not waste it. Water is as precious as gold. Let us learn to make compost to fertilize our soil. Do not wait for perfect conditions to plant. Develop a year round plan for your farms so that you can have crop to ensure revenue for you and your community. We must cease being one season farmers. That has not worked for us in the past. That is still not working now and is more than likely not going to work in the future. We have to be smart with our resources and gain more yield from our lands that we have in the past. Haiti must open herself up to revolutionary agricultural practices in parts of the world that will work in her climates. There is ample information out there to boost our agrarian industry to become a revenue maker for our economy.

When you live far from your girlfriend, you can say, for example, *honey, I am waiting for you like a farmer who waits for the rain* or *honey, I am dying to see you.* So, our farmers work only during the raining season, in a seeming love affair with the rain. However, reality does not agree with such fantasy because we have the whole country to feed every day. To get our daily bread we must cease this cycle of waiting for perfect conditions. Supplemental irrigation of our land must continue as a permanent feature of our farming. This information already exists. We only need to learn them. There are many problems in Haiti but we can solve them and bring water to the top of our mountains. People must decide to spend less time on violence and demonstration on the street and spend more time thinking about solving problems and creating jobs. Let us break away from false leaders who prod us to demonstrate and become rich from our ignorance. In 2012, we wasted energy. Haiti had about 400 protests. However, Haitian people are not violent at all. All bad behaviors are dirty pictures of any country and cast it in very bad light. When Haitians do any wrongdoing, it is like taking a handgun and firing at Haiti's feet. If you want Haiti to rise from the doldrums, you need to work hard, obey the laws and love the country. We must Haiti even though we do not share similar opinions. Our energies should be channeled towards the building of our individual, communal and national objectives. Let us remember the national motto: Union makes the force.

"O! Artibonite they called me
when I arrived I saw the sun was sick,

even though you still have plenty of tears to cry for Haiti."

Artibonite is the biggest river in the Caribbean area. Well, we need to have "kitanago" (solidarity) to carry water to every corner of Haiti. One business that generates billions in the world is water. Water is the most important element for nature, life or health. Our bodies need water to live. We find water everywhere but we cannot take it for granted. We must not waste water. It is invaluable. Let us plant trees for much rain to fall. We need water we drink. The water we used for bathing. The water for gardens that beautify our country. Let us change our relationship with water. One thing we can do is invite Israeli technicians to help us managed water better and sell the rest abroad. This will help us irrigate lands on the banks of the Artibonite land and sell the remaining water to the rest of the Caribbean. Artibonite is well-known as the biggest river in the Caribbean. We need tourists to come to visit it.

The land is our mother. We should feed her if we love her. Her food is water, manure and compost. Since we love the earth, we have to plant many trees to protect the soil. As we cover our bodies with clothing or blankets to protect ourselves or to feel comfortable, the earth itself needs plants for protection. If you use compost to make your food products, they will be products of the best quality and world-renowned. We send a belated congratulation to the Haitian government for making 2013 the year of reforestation. At the same time we should teach the Haitian people, especially school students, how to make or prepare compost.

When we begin to respect the value of available resources, we begin to give ourselves the opportunity of using them to our benefit. There are solutions to the most basic of our problems but we must build socio-economic platforms strong enough to contain those solutions. Efforts should be made in educating people about water and its absolute importance to development. Everyone should be involved in the preservation of our natural resources because they are our collateral against adversity.

6 - We should not start any wild fire.

Either you think, or else others have to think for you and take power from you, pervert and discipline your natural tastes, civilize and sterilize you.
- F. Scott Fitzgerald

We should stop burning our fields in preparation for the rain. This practice is so counterproductive that it has to stop immediately. By burning our fields, we sabotage our future ability to grow crops. We destroy the landscapes and vegetation, making it easier for erosion to occur whenever it rains. Fire is meant to be used to boil food, not to scorch the earth as an agricultural practice. We must stop practices that are widely accepted but have been found to be detrimental to our progress. We cannot allow culture to impede development. For our traditions to be relevant, they have to help us progress and not otherwise.

In the fifth section of Verrettes County, where I was born, peasants in the mountains, from late February to March, prepare the land in hopes for rainfall in April or May. Part of the preparation is to start fire everywhere. The habitations are razed to the ground. I must add that, sometimes in late December to early January, there are large brush fires on both sides of the Artibonite River. They last for several days. We usually say that it is the drunken people and cock fighters who start the fires, so they can see their way home, in the absence of the full moon.

When you burn the earth, you are destroying the food for the birds. You are burnings birdhouse, branches, leaves and grasses. You are literally burning our sustenance. Moreover, it is criminal act to burn a brush fire. This causes accelerated erosion. Because the earth is stripped naked by the fires, any passing rainfall can cause an avalanche and hauled down to the sea everything in its path.

So when we work our fields, we need to replace the bad and poor soil with compost for more output. We must cover the nakedness of our plants with tree leaves to help the phenomenon that is called condensation to keep our florae cool. We can also revert to the use of grass and any other waste to make fertilizer.

Starting fires do more harm than good to our vegetation. We can create fertilizer out of what we cut, thereby enriching our soils with nutrients. The call to responsible action starts from the individual to the society. We cannot wait for anyone to do the right thing. We must do the right thing. In the motion of destiny, each act is a step forward or a step back. The cumulative effort in stepping forward positions our nation at the cusp of prosperity.

7 - In cooperation with local authorities, we must create small forest communal places wherever it is possible.

We should not forget that it will be just as important to our descendants to be prosperous in their time as it is to us to be prosperous in our time.
- Theodore Roosevelt

Trees make rain and protect the underground water. Due to the power we give our state authorities, they are responsible for the wellbeing and prosperity of society. Our authorities are not different from us. We should not always think that we have to fight with them, in order to get results. They are members of society, just like us, but they have bigger responsibilities in leading the country on paths of development. But the authority cannot exist if there is no mutual respect for each other. After all we say out here, it is really important for us to respect our authorities and work with them. We can get reason with our authorities and organize ourselves to develop our communities. Let us make associations to help the state achieve what is necessary for the country. We need a partnership to solve every problem and to create jobs. There are problems that require the involvement of officials with more power. Today, we are facing a very serious problem of deforestation and our water fountains are drying. These are some of the many situations where highly-placed elected officials can help us in achieving an important objective. We cannot have responsible authority when we undermine their efforts with acts of disobedience. Our duty is to assist authorities in doing what is right for the community. Our relationship (with authorities) must be one of synergy. It should make the country fluid its efforts towards progress. Whereas it is on the authorities to serve the supreme interests of the people, the people must act in a way that complements their work. We are all children of Haiti. We fall when she falls. We rise when she rises. We cannot allow petty differences to stand in the way of purpose.

We would like to see a series of manmade forests with fruit trees like mangoes that can be exported. We should feed ourselves and bring into Haiti many export dollars. Let us identify the places that make coffee and coffee products. We must invest in them. We can encourage Haitian people to restart the planting of coffee. We must research and plant crops with high yield and demand. It is important to position ourselves as an essential supplier of something the world needs.

We cannot exist in void, insulating ourselves against others. We must collaborate with fellow Haitians, especially those in government, to push reforestation in our communities. This action will mitigate the effects that centuries of brush fires have had on our forests. By conducting reforestation, we will be able to lessen the impact of rainfalls on our land by the retention of top soil nutrients. We need to reclaim the forests, just as we are reclaiming our destiny as a nation, by planting trees that will be beneficial to us in the future.

8 - We should consult with local and national authorities on how we can begin to find other energy sources to replace wood and charcoal.

Knowledge is power. Information is liberating. Education is the premise of progress, in every society, in every family.
-Kofi Annan (former UN Secretary-General)

The principal energy sources that we use in Haiti today are wood or charcoal. This practice is also undermining the country. We nearly cut all the trees to cook our food and more. This leads to a total deforestation of the country. Cutting trees is a practice that destroys life. We see that in each rainfall that comes pouring down. Trees have a secret beauty of love. At the same time, they protect the soil and prevent erosion Trees give us oxygen to breathe. Need I say more? Why can we find other sources of energy to replace wood and charcoal in Haiti?

Without question, energy is the lynchpin of development and the nation that ignores it, ignores it at her own peril. Haiti has to come up with a modern plan of development in the energy sector. We cannot depend on wood and charcoal to be our energy sources if we seek to attract investment. We need strategic partnerships that will bring us to par on dependable energy sources that will open business opportunities for communities that have none. The solution to this problem is a top national priority that should be handled not out of partisan score-keeping but through patriotic fervor. Energy cannot be put on the back burner and excused away as one of those things to be tackled in the distant future. We need to begin work in this sector as soon as possible.

Energy has to become a top priority for our nation. When it is handled deftly, a floodgate of opportunities will present itself. Our nation should partner with other nations with experience and expertise in the creation of alternate energy. An African proverb states that *what is necessary is done before what is aesthetic.* Energy, far more than any superficial need, is a critical part of our development as a nation.

The game is almost over. But you do not change players when a team is winning. In our case, we must play the game with extraordinary focus. This is because we will all disappear if we do not seek in cooperation with local and national governments to find other energy sources to replace wood and charcoal. One of the possibilities we have is to start investing in the so-called renewable energy. It is beautiful and clean. You can count on it and it is not expensive. We get renewable energy from the sun, wind, water, natural gas et cetera. We must state in passing that Haiti is a country rich in natural resources. Thus one of the first energy source we think Haiti should seek to exploit is the sun, we should use it to produce electricity and for cooking et cetera. Alternatively, we should construct many hydroelectric. Let us all enter into negotiations with the authorities and also with the private sector with respect, order and discipline to create a fund grants for college studies to begin forming many technicians in this new field of renewable energy so we can stop cutting down trees and prevent avalanche which brings us and all we have at sea and, Haiti will return the pearl of islands again.

9 - We should control our power to make babies.

You can have it all. Just not all at once.
- Oprah Winfrey

We should not spend on things that are not necessary, we must practice prevention that we can live healthy. Family planning can help young children finished school and to be successful; it helps families decide when to have another child again. When two people decide to have a child, this child comes as a blessing to that family. When we control ourselves, when we are prepared before having kids, their development is guaranteed. Our families will always be in good health. If the Haitian people stick to birth control, Haiti will become a healthy country where people invest their time and treasure in requirements for a better life. This will help us save money, which can be invested in small businesses.

Avoidance is better than asking forgiveness. Let us begin to working in collaboration with our authorities and the rest of the society to prevent the diseases before they wipe us out. For example, malaria has oppressed our Haiti for a long time. What gives us malaria is the perpetual breeding of mosquitoes from dirty puddles. Let us keep the areas where we live clear of waste and puddles. Starvation, stomach ache or hunger is the conditions that most people in Haiti live in. To prevent these uncomfortable conditions in our neighborhoods, let us produce more food on large scales year round. We can eat all the time if we open ourselves to knowledge, awareness and the technology needed to liberate us from poverty. Until we find ways to preempt catastrophe, we will be its perpetual victims.

There is an American theory of 5 Ps: *Prior preparation prevents poor performance*. The joy that babies bring is priceless but they come with hefty price tags. In our current economic problems, family planning is critical to our progress as individuals and communities. We have to find a way to space our children so that they will not drain our ability to provide for them. A child born into poverty becomes a drag on the family's finances, rendering them incapable of entering businesses that need startup capital. The objective here is to have a strategy when it comes to having children. It is proper to balance the dreams of prosperity and the need for posterity. I also know that in agrarian communities children are needed on the farm. The more children one has, the more hands one has on the farm. I bring this particular subject up because I have seen, at first hand, how the lack of family planning has derailed the dreams of many industrious farmers.

The essence of responsible behavior is a must where the objective is change. We must channel our energies not only into reproduction but into restoring our communities. We must first build our world to become a platform on which our children can succeed. We are at a place of national destiny where we should not be afraid to destroy and rebuild our socio-economic foundations. Preparation is better than living by ad hoc measures. Prevention is better than atonement. We must create a world that welcomes our young, not the kind that destroys their dreams.

10 - **We must educate our children and teach them how to create a job or find one.**

Every man should make his son or daughter learn some useful trade or profession, so that in these days of changing fortunes of being rich today and poor tomorrow they may have something tangible to fall back upon. This provision might save many persons from misery, who by some unexpected turn of fortune have lost all their means.
- P. T Barnum

We should teach our kids to work or participate in small business to pay their school fees. This instills a sense of responsibility and appreciation for the education they are getting. They can learn how to manage their lives at an early age. This can help us change the culture of dependence to that of work and production. Where everyone considers work as a sacred duty, it results in positive socio-economic consequences. To dispose of all complexes that make us think, we rather sit playing dominoes until we found an office job.

People think that, after going to school, they cannot work the soil. The assumption is that the work is beneath them. This is a sad disposition to opportunities begging to be taken. The irony is that that very disposition crumbles when Haitians crossed the border and reach Miami. You have to take the first job you can get, which is usually washing dishes or cleaning the floor. Now how is that different from farm work? We hope one day, the Haitian immigrants in the USA can make life a little easier by telling their relatives the stark truth.

When you are given a job in the USA, you give it your all. Since you are in a job waiting to be taken by three or four people, you have to work very hard to keep it.

Even when you feel very tired, you cannot stop. If you stop, you will lose your job. If you do not work, you cannot pay your bills. Hence, it is possible to become homeless and sleep under bridges. Imagine being homeless in the snow. So the Haitian immigrant in the USA has to work hard and obey the laws. That is the only way they can feed themselves and their families back home in Haiti.

I believe that, in addition to a good education, every child needs to learn a vocation. I remember in 2007, when the American financial system crashed, friends with vocations (like auto mechanics) had steady jobs while those with desk jobs were laid off. That was a cautionary tale of how important it was to have every student learn a trade as well. Haiti will do itself a favor if it invests in after-school vocational training for high school and college students. With the education, coupled with vocational training, that student is more likely to become a small business owner. Haiti must push her young in the right direction. Our educational system must be recalibrated to feed the demands of this century. We must arm our students with the necessary training so that they will be ready for opportunities that come their way. Haiti must train her students to be doers and go-getters. We must inculcate into them that everything is possible when the heart is full of perseverance. Let us invest in our schools and vocational institutions to fashion our students into powerhouses of talents in high demand in this century.

Finally, I am going to share with you my own little bit of truth. To hear and to see are two different things. Leaving Haiti to go on vacation overseas and immigration are not the same. I was lucky to visit the U.S. several times before I decided to stay in 2002. My first job was to sweep, mop and wash dishes. However, before I left Haiti, I worked for the government and several NGOs. I also went to university in France. I met many people and made the best out of my life. I learned very quickly, that in advanced countries, you are responsible for how your life turns out. You go out and get a job. You work hard and save enough to take care of any extra needs. You go to school to get certifications and advanced degrees to give yourself more opportunities in the world. You get an idea and, if you do your homework well, you can go out on a limb and create a small business. That is why the saying, the sky is the limit, is true in the advanced world. I hope this little sharing can help the Haitian people to drop their complex and start doing whatever job they can lay their hands on. This change in attitude is instrumental to a new dispensation for our beloved Haiti.

The concept of employment must change. The youth must be told in clear terms that as long as they have skills, they should not wait to be employed, in order to put them to use. The ability to take risks and the necessity of confidence in one's dreams should be instilled in the young. They must be reminded that they are at the driving seat of their own success. I understand that not everyone can run a business by themselves but everyone can be in a business like it is theirs. The mentality wherein people expect to be saved, without doing anything to save themselves, must change. The attitude towards work must be self-propelled, not in reaction to external pressures.

In the United States, it is of critical importance to be employed because one's ability to stay afloat depends on that. We sell ourselves short, in Haiti, when we are choosy about opportunities in a country where there is virtually none. We must be humble enough to start somewhere even if it is lower than what we have envisioned. There is a basic rule about opportunities: you make them or you take them. In America, there is an axiom that most people are two paychecks away from being homeless. Work and comfort go hand in hand. The loss of one results in the loss of the other. When it comes to work, we have no choice. Human existence is premised on work. Everything (thoughts, words and actions) is work.

11 - We must maintain the area where we live (and our country) well.

If the human race wishes to have a prolonged and indefinite period of material prosperity, they have only got to behave in a peaceful and helpful way towards each other.
- Winston Churchill

We must opt to live in sanitary conditions. We live in houses. We live on the streets and in a country. If we keep those three areas uncontaminated, we will have healthy lives. It will gain us have more respect from tourists. It is extremely important for us to stay in a house with no filth. A dirty house is a factory of diseases. Germs are friends with dirt, filth is where microbes multiply. If you live in a clean house, you will live longer. Environment is critical to the sustenance of health. We will not get sick for any reason. Such a positive change in sanitation will not make us prone to infection. The key to health and prosperity is a focus on sanitation. Good health protects wealth. Medical bills can make you poor in a moment. Just as we need air, our homes need to better management. They say cleanliness is next to godliness. We take charge of our destiny when we pay attention to the simple things.

The street is the living room of the people. We heard about this on the lips of all Haitians. The living room, where we relax, is also where we welcome our visitors. The street is ours to maintain. It is also the first thing foreign visitors see when they come to our country. Hence, since no one leaves dirt in the living room, our streets should not be left filthy. We must leave that practice of dumping in ditches or streets when rain falls. We need to find solutions for slum areas. To keep Haiti clean, the government and all of society must find a replacement solution for slums. One of them is that people living in slums have to be relocated to better managed areas. This will give government and private investors the ability to clean them up and restore the aesthetic value. We should continue to keep the countryside clean to be used as a model for the cities. For example, one of the important actions we must take as a nation is to create jobs and housing in rural areas. This is to modernize the standard of living in Haiti. The present living conditions are so bad that the country people would not move in slums. It is possible move people living in the slums back to live where they used to live in the countryside.

Countries outside become favorable for thousands of Haitians because of hard work, obedience to the law and love of humanity. Those countries are kept clean and are strict about enforcing laws about slum housing. If they can do it and make themselves attractive to immigrants, why can't we do it in our own nation? Let us create a new environment that offers everyone a better life.

We should not expect government to come and remind us to keep our environs clean. It is paramount to our image to have clean communities. More important than image, is the issue of health. We cannot treat our environment the way we like and expect to be disease free. Garbage in, garbage out. If we keep our communities clean, it will result in fewer incidents of outbreaks. If we don't, we will have no one to blame for the epidemics that ensue. There is an English proverb that goes, your home is your castle. If our homes are our castles, then why are they filthy? What are they looking messy? The way we treat our environments is the way people will treat us. Wolove emphasizes on the work part because without it, we will not see the development we badly seek. Besides, if we cannot keep what we already have, how can we maintain anything new? We must challenge ourselves to become good stewards of Haiti. She deserves better.

It is true that there is no other country in the Caribbean that has most potential in tourism than Haiti. It is true also that the Haitian government and the tourism minister (Ms. Stephanie B.V.) are doing a wonderful job to promote tourism. To complement what the government is doing, the Haitian people must work on their own to clean Haiti and keep it clean. It would be good to embark on a national campaign to keep reminding people to keep Haiti clean. This should be done in schools, churches, radio and television. We will never stop repeating this narrative. One man's waste can become another man's treasure. We must decide to collect and sort waste in the country and recycle them into objects that can be useful to the society. The knowhow exists already. We only need the will to learn. Let me tell you about an incident that happen to me at the Saint Baume forest in France. I went to the forest with a French friend. We ate and fraternized. At a point, I threw the aluminum foil that wrapped the gum I was chewing on the ground. Friends, I was reprimanded. My act could destroy the forest because the waste that I threw down was not biodegradable. I had to pick the foil up and place it in a dumpster nearby.

In France, as in most developed countries, people do not spit or urinate everywhere they like. In the United States of America, people are fined up to $1,000 for littering. This shows how serious they are about the idea of clean communities. We cannot be lackadaisical about our environs and expect a clean bill of health. Our attitude towards dirt must change. We should require cleanliness in our homes, counties and countries. This, in itself, creates job opportunities. Our environment is a reflection of our national psyche. It is a glimpse into priorities we have, as a nation. A community in disarray does not attract respect. By extension, it does not attract visitors. We must make cleanliness a priority for our communities

12 - We must build portable and durable places of convenience.

Self-respect is the fruit of discipline; the sense of dignity grows with the ability to say no to oneself.
- Abraham Joshua Heschel

In the new Haiti we are building together; we should not waste anything. Let us save and transform our waste, be it human, animal and vegetation, into compost and cooking gas. We must utilize the best modern techniques to save and reuse our waste. To begin this process, we should stop using deep latrine systems because we lose the excrements, which end up contaminating our water sources. We should not defecate on the ground either. Flies may rest on the turds and contaminate our fruits, vegetables and all other foods that we eat.

Every community has to build well-sanitized places of convenience as a priority. We have to invest time and money in ensuring that human waste does not become a launch pad for diseases in our communities. Modern technological advances exist that offer efficient ways of handling human waste. We have to research and find the system that works best in our climates. The health sector holds a lot of opportunities for innovators in the private sector and the universities.

We need to do our homework to find out if there is any system out there that can help us in this particular regard. We can also ask our universities to develop toilet systems that are environmentally safe. That invention can be a money maker for them. I remember in 1997, at the time that I was going to leave France to come back to live in Haiti definitely, I experienced something profound with a group of French intellectuals who had left their comfortable life to return to the campaign, to become farmers. Their mission was to tame and transform arid lands. They decided to share their time, experience and expertise with other farmers throughout the world. One of their models is a hygienic toilet that does not use septic tanks. It is designed in a way that the water and feces from the bathroom are channeled into the land to fertilize it. They also planted a special kind of grass that fed on the microbes in the fecal matter. In a short time, the project areas were blooming with vegetation.

13 - **We must treat water with respect.**

Responsibility is the price of freedom.
- Elbert Hubbard

Water is life. Water covers ¾ of the earth. We humans are 80% water. Our relationship with water ought to be protective. We cannot be careless about water. It feeds us. It cleanses us. Our communities have to pay more attention to the sanitary conditions of water in our areas. We should not tolerate any act that desecrates our water bodies. We should educate our people on modern ways with which we all can become good stewards of the water bodies in our areas.

Today, we believe that no one in Haiti can ignore how important it is for us to have good drinking water. After all, we remember the damage that cholera did in our society when thousands of people died in a very short period of time. It was alleged that the disease was brought by a group of

UN soldiers in Haiti. We should get in the habit of drinking boiled or treated water. Let us value the importance of water by stopping the cutting of trees. Planting trees instead will give us access to an abundance of water. When everybody treats water, by way of example, we can reinvent a clean country. Haiti can become a motherland that produces clean drinking water that can give us revenue on the international market. Water is the most cherished treasure on the earth for all life. Without water, there is no life. If someone does not drink for a long time, he/she will die. Water is the backbone of health. Haiti, land of the brave! Haiti, people of character! Let educate ourselves and place ourselves on track to socio-economic development. Haiti can once again become the Perl of islands.

14 - **We should not spend too much money on marital rites.**

There is scarcely anything that drags a person down like debt.
- P.T Barnum

I want to share with you a personal experience that I had in the Baptist (Tòtòy/Haiti) area in the early 1990s. Tòtòy is a fertile area where many types of crops such as corn, coffee and beans are grown. People in the area could be very generous to a fault, especially during marriage rites. This practice reduces their savings. As an illustration, when two young people plan to marry, the groom's parents begin to build a house for the couple. On the other hand, the bride's parents buy all kinds of furniture to furnish that house. After the wedding, the parents continue to take care of the young couple. I do not have any problem in giving a good gift to someone who is getting married. But marriage is wonderful, if and only if, the two people who are getting married are prepared. If the couple cannot care for themselves, they are not ready to be married.

Marriage is a beautiful event, a milestone in the lives of a couple. However, it should not become a drain on our finances. It is not a must to hold lavish ceremonies. We know that marriage is not what happens on the first day but in the subsequent ones. Let us focus on making marriages work by ensuring financial stability. Let us not waste money on one day they will definitely forget when the going gets tough for them. The objective of this suggestion is to encourage responsibility in our community. The couple has to be responsible for their marriage and the costs that come with it. The families of the bride and groom ought to find a way to channel the money into something that will ensure financial stability for the couple. There has to be sea change in how we spend money in our communities. We cannot encourage waste and expect to stay wealthy. It will be helpful to the couple, and the community at large, for the families' to grant soft loans for business when they wed. This exacts responsibility from the couple. Marriage is a journey, not a destination.

When we decided to marry and not have a job or a thriving business, we only add more variables to calculations of poverty. Well, my friends you can spend on the wedding as you want if you have the means. We must also know that in life, chances are the result of hard work. The game is in your hand. You can decide what is best for you and for your fatherland.

15 - We must not abuse others.

When you are content to be simply yourself and don't compare or compete, everyone will respect you.
- Lao Tzu

The manner we conduct ourselves is the very manner people respond to us. There is absolutely no need to be obnoxious in your community. As poet Maya Angelou said, hatred creates all of the problems in the world but has not been able to give us one solution. In the quest for development, we must appeal to our higher angels and leave bickering behind. What did not work in the past is not going to work today or in the future. Let us put aside our differences and focus on a mutually beneficial future. We cannot allow pettiness to stand in the way of our development. We cannot excuse division to be present as we plot the chart to a shared destiny. We must learn to forgive and forget, for Haiti's sake. We leave the motivations to pull our neighbor down and channel our energy into pulling him up.

You must not trample the rights of another person under feet. You should not allow someone else to abuse other people. It is an injustice to punish people for they have not done or be prejudiced on the basis of identity. "Injustice anywhere is a threat for Justice Everywhere" (Martin Luther King, Jr.) As injustice affect every layer in Haitian society, it will be difficult for us to talk about 1 specific aspects of injustice in the country. I will tackle general injustice in Haiti. For example, take an individual, who is allegedly well bred, and put him/her in one of the protests in the streets of Haiti where everyone is unruly. He/she is more likely to burn rubber or destroy property, like everybody else. This individual will participate in the same behavior as the group. However, if you remove this morally individual from the group and you would give him/her diamonds to repeat the same things he was saying in the group, they would not repeat the words.

Nobody is responsible enough, especially when nobody is looking. We are all guilty of varying levels of narcissism. The absence of a national education plan is the worst injustice in Haiti. This is the platform needed for Haiti's emergence as a powerhouse of ideas, services and products. We have to rebuild our nation into a place the love of education is paramount. Government must encourage communal efforts to morph Haiti into a world of love and beauty. The time we spend in criticizing another and government is a waste of time. It is time that can go into the start or completion of something constructive. Very often, we say that government is stealing our money. But, have not we ever paused to ask ourselves the following questions: where does the money to pay state employees come from? In all working societies, State employees or members of the government are paid by the people's taxes. For Haiti, more than 60% of the national budget is from international loans and donor support. It is time for Haitians, at home and abroad, to brainstorm ways to change this image. This must stop. Perhaps our rulers do not deserve the criticism. They can only work with what they have and, if it is meager, they have to make do. If we learn to respect our authorities and work with them to find solutions to our problems, we will begin to see results.

We do not believe that our leaders are the worst in the world. Rather, our leaders, like the rest of society, are victims of a system that does not work well. A country is a demarcated land mass with people with a common cause and destiny working collectively to bring prosperity and welfare. Haiti is a place where everyone tends to be individualistic. This attitude hinders progress, especially as we seek to create a new education system to reinvent Haitian into a vibrant country in a modern world. For the creation of a new Haitian society, we must plot our national development blueprint that spans 20 to 40 years. Every citizen must be engaged in bring this set of plans to pass. Examples of such national determination abound. In China, due to an emphasis on educational opportunity, more citizens have become very prosperous. Education has helped in lifting more than 300 million people in China from poverty in less than twenty-five years. Education is the best remedy against poverty. One way we can educate ourselves is to ask your neighbors and friends all over the world to teach us what they already know. Education is a major tool. It is like a supernatural power that moves the mountains of impossibility. Education can take us out of lack to a path of prosperity similar to that of the United States. It has the ability to lift us up to higher pedestals in life.

16 - **We must join together to make big investments.**

There is only one thing that makes a dream impossible to achieve: the fear of failure.
- Paulo Coelho

We must make major investments that we may generate revenue. We should also learn how to protect the money we already have. This will enable us to provide many job opportunities. It is not possible for every Haitian peasant to be a small farmer and a street vendor, at the same time. Big investments can transform our standard of living and create sustainable jobs. People like to invest in countries that are serious about their own development. Let us make a series of major social investments in rural areas. The nation must build infrastructure to assist in the production and restoration of goods for local and international markets. This new attitude should help Haitians to feel good about themselves anywhere they go. Slum living would be a thing of the past. In this time of need, the Haitian State should set goals, together with the private sector, to make roads, channel water and provide electricity. Communication is the basis of development. We should gather farmers and investors in a marketplace of ideas to help them produce and sell goods on site. Let us learn to invest together to develop our country.

The sea is a collection of water drops. One person with a dollar can only purchase something of a dollar's worth. A collective of one hundred people, each with a dollar, can purchase something worth a hundred dollars. Community, when focused on a good objective, has the power to change its trajectory. We must build trust and faith in each other to fund our own development. We do not need outside donors to do everything for us, just as we do not need government for everything. We have, within us, all it takes to maximize the opportunities that lie before us. A community that thinks this way will build itself quickly into a powerhouse of opportunity for its members. We have to brainstorm solutions to the problems at hand by having the knowledge to reach informed decisions.

17 - We must develop small supermarket home teams so we do not buy or sell our agricultural products on dirty floors in old market halls.

The future belongs to those who believe in the beauty of their dreams.
-   Eleanor Roosevelt

We must not buy anything to eat if it is not displayed in the best hygienic condition. Our cities are not dumping sites. It is time to start reorganizing small farmers and business merchants in mutual beneficial cooperatives.

Haiti is an agrarian country. We must produce and sell our products in some new ways. We must work, in cooperation with public and private sectors, to set up an agricultural bank that provides lines of credit to our farmers for the purchase of quality seeds. Alternatively, there should be a group of companies who buy the products and distribute them on national and international markets. We should help local communities in the creation of clean mini supermarkets.

Let our rulers find ways to detect scams so that they can make everyone pay taxes without fail. Let us treat everyone equal before the law, from the president to the peasants. Together with our authorities, we can start a development plan work towards the day Haiti can handle its issues without asking for charity abroad. Rather than having every Haitian as a small planter or trader, we will create a service industry that caters to the needs of the other industries. For example, if 200 farmers from the same area yields potato products, we should seek to create a cooperative will buy the potato and market it for them. Everyone will have money to buy food in nice restaurants or buy new clothes in beautiful shops. In this new Haiti we are inventing, there will no need to buy used or dirty clothing from other countries. Finally, we of Wolove are ready to disseminate whatever information we have with any person or group of people who want to develop our ideas for change in Haiti.

18 - **We must be ready to help support each other.**

The battle of life, in most cases, fought uphill; and to win it without a struggle were perhaps to win it without honor. If there were no difficulties there would be no success; if there were nothing to struggle for, there would be nothing to be achieved.
- Samuel Smiles.

In a country like Haiti, money talks. It is not enough to have good ideas. Money has to partner with ideas to make things happen. It was in that spirit that we started our own little credit line called: *Wolove Small Credit Solidarity*. The model is simple yet effective. We kick started the various small businesses within our group with soft loans and credit management training. There are no small businesses with minor or major credit lines. Most of the jobs we see in the U.S. come from 26 million small businesses. But because small businesses in Haiti are not sustained by a financial backbone, they do not have the ability to contribute effectively to the prosperity of the Haitian economy. We must learn these things from our America friends: the English language, customer service skills and small business management training. Each Wolove group has about 3 to 5 members. We should group with people that we know and trust. People with vested interest in our success. We must become model citizens of our nation. Wolove members operate on ethics and scruples that help us distinguish ourselves in the conduct of business. We must not kill. We shall not steal.

With the *Wolove* concept, we must love everyone as we love ourselves. We must treat everyone with love and respect. We have to keep smiling and say: *hello, thank you, please or excuse me* etc. Friends, you ought to congratulate and encourage others for achieving things in life, regardless of who they are. If there is anybody who has a problem we all should help him/her solve it.

19 - We must participate in community work.

Discipline is the bridge between goals and accomplishment.
- Jim Rohn

Scholars have said that people should not live alone. Everyone is a social subject. People are effective when they live in communities. We must understand that our communities represent us before the world. When visitors come to visit us, they see the collective before the individual. This means that our faces and the face of the community are one. This is why the members of a community should be working all the time to keep it beautiful. When we are doing construction work in our communities we should not do it anyhow. We should observe construction rules pre-established by our authorities that state where we can build and where we cannot build. Let us develop, in cooperation with Haitian banks, home building companies that make affordable homes for sale or homes for rent. When we speak of a house, we talk about the kind that meets international standards. The work for the future starts now.

No one is above communal labor. We must encourage everyone in the community to participate in keeping it clean. It belongs to us all. It is our reflection to the rest of the world.

20 – Let all be happy.

Feeling sorry for yourself, and your present condition, is not only a waste of energy but the worst habit you could possibly have.
- Dale Carnegie

Maintain a healthy outlook, people. Now that we decided to work together for the welfare and prosperity of all, we must act without delay. It is time to synergize ourselves into forces of development. There is joy and hope in sticking together. In all socio-economic activities we undertake, we must leave room for socialization. Happiness is most effective medication. Let us give ourselves, and our society, a dose of joy wherever we find ourselves. Let us laugh until we break the chains that hold us down. May the beauty of love invade us all. Our house must be clean and beautiful. We should rejoice together and seek happiness without denying somebody else's. There is a divine remedy for existential malaise. Its name is joy. We are here to create the aura with joy in the world. For this, we must give the gift of learning what works in the nations we admire. This is why we began *Wolove* and *iFriendnett.org* as platforms to learn English for free and change our lives for the better. The English language is a tool of communication that allows you to learn a lot online. Command of the language opens a universe of free training in any business under the sun. If you are happy, you will be a good friend to yourself, your community and your nation.

Happiness is contingent on you. You have to make that choice. No one can force you to be happy. However, you remove the burdens of the world, one day at a time, by deciding to be happy. Happiness is an inside job. It is not driven by what happens on the outside. It is in the confidence we have in ourselves that, if we keep doing what is necessary, we shall see great results. *Wolove* is a set of ideas that thrive on happiness. Work and happiness. Obedience and happiness. Love and happiness. We lift our heads up, out of the sands of sorrow and smile in the sunlight of life. We can do whatever we set our minds on. The path to destiny has been shown. The decision is up to us.

Let us remember that, in our idealism, we must not forget reality. The reality is that in a place of abject poverty, the motivation is not to work towards a great future. Instead, it is to survive the burdens of circumstance. It is difficult to explain a dream set in the future to a hungry man. He is more likely to listen on a full stomach. This immediacy fights the careful structuring of the future. There is always a fight between what the world should be and what the world is. I am cognizant of this fact. However, we have to set the ball rolling, in order to attain the commitment of the willing.

According to Pareto's principle, eighty per cent of work is done by twenty percent of the work force. This is insightful, in that it tells us that a few determined members of a community can move it in the right direction. Strength has always been in numbers but success lies in knowing what must be done. Haiti needs a group of dedicated citizens who are prepared to lead by example. It needs people who are not fazed by circumstances and who find solutions amid problems.

OBEY THE LAWS

Kay koule twonpe solèy, men li pa ka twonpe lapli.

A leaking house (roof) might fool the sun, but cannot fool the rain.

(Haitian Proverb)

Haiti is a country of laws. In cities and towns, we have the police and the court systems. But there are parts of the country, called the outside, where conviction and respect for each other do not exist. Nobody can ignore the law. It is the law that controls what we can do and cannot do. The duty and responsibility of the authorities is to enforce the law. This means that we, in civil society, should have good relationships with our authorities. We must work hand in hand with our establishments to change the face of Haiti. Let us pay taxes on time and participate no more in corrupt practices. The essence of law has two things of great importance: the exercise of our rights and the performance of our duties. The rights of people help them to live in peace. Your rights end where the rights of others begin.

Everyone must respect the law. A country is truly great when her citizens take their civic duties seriously.

No man is above the law and no man is below it: nor do we ask any man's permission when we ask him to obey it.
- Theodore Roosevelt

Our fathers fought for our political freedom. Today, it has fallen on us to fight in harmony with other people in the world who seek socio-economic freedom. John F. Kennedy, one of the great American presidents, said: "Ask not what your country can do for you – ask what you can do for your country." In 1997, in a town called Montpellier, France, there were about 700 associations where French citizens had come together to help their communities move in areas where government had overlooked. We must be a people of mission. Days and nights of working closely with authorities can transform Haiti into a paradise for ourselves and vacationers from all over the world. To be successful with the small businesses that we create, we need 3 things. The first one is education. The second is education and the third is also education. The government should borrow money and add it to our tax money to build roads, channel water, provide electricity, introduce technology and erect schools. This can be done while starting a community that deals with goods and services. We can invite foreign businessmen to come and invest in our tourism industry. Our project is already half successful because we already know what to do. We already know where we are going and what we want. We only need the resources to start. The law is a structure that molds society to remain reliable. Its success depends on honest, productive citizens. I remember what my friend Lenji told me one day: when you pour water on a flat surface it scattered in all directions. But when you put water in a pipe, it takes the shape of the pipe.' This means that we all walk in the Haitian standard of righteousness. Let us obey the laws so that we can live in harmony in a beautiful Haiti where everyone has the desire to live and *Wolove* each other.

Obedience is neither docility nor subservience. Obedience is a sign of respect for the laws that govern us. We humans exist on laws. Physical laws. Moral laws. Biological Laws. Constitutional Laws. Family Laws et cetera. You name the field and there are laws that govern that field. Obedience is the active recognition of the importance of laws in our lives. We obey because we want to be connected to synergy of community. We obey because we desire to reap the wages of good citizenry. We obey because we want our society to be the best environment for our families and loved ones to flourish in. We are called to be part of the miracle called life. Obedience is the price we pay for being part of life. Without law and order, anarchy will run roughshod through our land. We all know that anarchy has never developed anything. We cannot tolerate attitudes and actions that fight against our progress as a nation.

The United States of America thrives on the rule of law where each and every one has a reasonable expectation of fairness from the court system. Even when verdicts do not go the way of popular opinion, people have the decency to accept them. This is obedience in action. This shows that the people will not allow one bad decision to destroy all that is good about their society. I have the utmost respect for the American people for their obedience to the laws. Of course, there are bad nuts but the majority thrives on the attitude of obedience. This is a wonderful example for Haiti to follow.

LOVE YOUR COUNTRY

Pa pèdi founo pou yon grenn pen.
Don't lose the oven for a piece of bread.
(Haitian Proverb)

Love someone is to help that person realize the greatest dream he/she has in life. Haiti is our motherland. It is a beautiful country. Thus, to like Haiti is to help Haiti become more beautiful. People are responsible for making the face of their country beautiful. You and your country are one. People tend to like your country if you like it too. If Haiti becomes beautiful and prosperous again, tourists from all over the world will visit. For example, most people on earth would like to visit the U.S.A one day. It is a country with a dream for all Americans that called the American dream. It is a dream that is the range of all. To attain the American dream is very easy. It is encapsulated in education plus hard work equal realization of your personal dream. Also, every American has a duty to their country and that includes working hard and helping neighbors. America is the number 1 that does its best to help change the world for the better. It is in this sense that we created iFriendnett.org worldwide, starting in the island of Kiskeya We help students and workers to learn English for free. We teach customer service and small business skills. Small businesses are the back bone of the U.S. economy, which is the world's number one.

To help Haiti become more prosperous, we suggest the practice of three ethical ideas of the American society that we fully endorse:

WO♥ - WOLOVE

The American Triangle of Success:

W (work hard),
O (obey the law),
♥ (love your country).

To show our love in our heart for our country, we must live the following principles:

1 - Love our Haiti like ourselves.

Loyalty to country always. Loyalty to government, when it deserves it.
- Mark Twain

The love for the country should be strong. It is patriotic love to do only what is beautiful and beneficial for one's Country. To keep us alert is to sing patriotic songs in our official ceremonies with our right hands on our hearts. Students and staff should accord reverence to the flag. Today this is with all our heart that we say: with hard work, our mind and knowledge we have a national plan before the international community to show we are serious. Let us fight to create a new Haitian who is intellectually in Haiti's service. We should be glad to let the other countries act in solidarity with our country. We live in an interrelated world. Haiti is where freedom rose against the abomination of slavery. Nevertheless, today's Haiti suffers and is still in labor. Nevertheless, Haiti is still in labor after 200 years. Our country is yet to encounter deliverance. Haiti needs a class wherein no color, race or religion plays a role in the revolution of the free knowledge. We must enlighten and help Haiti regain its place in the world as the mother of modern freedom.

2 - Celebrate national holidays with pride.

The duty of a patriot is to protect his country from its government.
- Thomas Paine

On national holidays, we celebrate the Haitian nation. We have many communities. Communities of peasants, drivers, physicians, educators, fishermen et cetera. National holidays bring these communities together to celebrate events special to our nation. People from all social layers join to celebrate. One of Haiti's national holidays is May 18, where we celebrate our flag. We gather under one flag, the blue and red, to celebrate freedom and our pride as a people.

Another national holiday we have is the January 1st, the Freedom Holiday. It is a day where we travel around the country to visit family and friends. We share gifts and eat a lot of pumpkin soup. I hope that one day, Haiti make provisions in our independence day celebrations for the Polish and German soldiers who fought by our side in the war against the French colonists. We understand that Emperor Dessalines wanted to see everyone free and equal. However, he did not want to tolerate the evil settlers who wanted to keep the abhorrent practice of chattel slavery. This explains that the emperor and other generals agreed to recognize German and Polish soldiers who helped us fight against slave traders. He gave that great group of soldiers the right to own land and live in Haiti. Their descendants live in Casale and Fond des Blancs today.

We are designed to be beautiful and to share that beauty with others. We should expand the framework of a shared culture and historical affiliation with Poles and Germans who helped us in the birth of the Haitian nation. They also spread liberty across the American continent by helping luminaries like Francisco de Miranda and Bolivar. It is time to share with you a version of the national anthem of our country, even if it is not really official:

For Haiti, the Ancestors' Country
We must walk hand in hand
There must not be traitors among us
We must be our own master.
Let's walk hand in hand for
Haiti can be more beautiful.
Let us, Let us put our heads together
For Haiti in the name of all the Ancestors.
For Haiti and for the Ancestors we must be able,
Valiant men are not born to serve other men.

This is why all parents must send their children to school to learn about the glorious acts of Toussaint, Dessalines, Christophe and Petion. There is a lot we can learn about Haiti by reading and understanding circumstances of our birth as a nation. We have to know who we are. We cannot accept the definitions of others as the final words on the destiny of our nation. It is important for Haitians to conduct this soul-searching. This will augment the suggestions I have listed in this book.

For Haiti in the name of the Ancestors
We must toil, we must sow
It is in the soil that all our strength sits
It is it that feeds us
Let us toil the soil, let us toil the soil
Joyfully, may the land be fertile
Mow, water, men like women
Must we come to live only by our arms' strength.

For Haiti in the name of the Ancestors
Let us raise our head and look above
Must everyone ask the Grandmaster
To grant us protection?
For evils may not turn us back
For we will march in the good path
For liberty be liberty
May justice cover the Nation.
We have a flag like all people
We must love it, die for it –
It was not a gift from the whites
It was our Ancestors' blood that flooded
We must keep our flag high

We must work, we must be together
For other countries to respect us
This flag is the soul of the Haitian People.

3 - **We must live *kombitologically***

The greatest patriotism is to tell your country when
it is behaving dishonorably, foolishly, viciously.
-   Julian Barnes (Flaubert's Parrot)

In the same way, like human been, the words are born, live, develop multiple meanings and die. Today is the turn of the Haitian's word *kombit*. We have a culture of oral tradition in Haiti. The sacred word, *kombit*, means *working together*. It has been in use for over 200 years. Members of the Wolove Small Credit Solidarity are asked to practice *kombitology*. *Kombitology* is a system that goes from feeding you to your education, from your education to your development in using a single circuit which is a lovely social relationship between everybody. I am talking about communal efforts towards the improvement of living conditions. It can be through education, farming or any effort that creates better standards of living for a community.

Together, we are stronger. It is the *kombit* idea that helps farmers to feed Haiti for over 200 years. For example, in Artibonite, ten poor peasants can put in collective labor for tilling or harvesting in field. The next day, they gather in another field until everyone's field gets its turn. Peasants without land come together to work so they can get money to survive. For example, five farmers, who have no land, come together to work the lands of other farmers, who have money to pay them? What happens is that all the money they earn in a day goes to the pocket of one person in the group. The next day, it goes to another person until everyone is paid. So far, *kombitology* remains a practice among Haitian peasants. It is a social philosophy that Haitian peasants have been practicing for over two centuries. We believe it is vital that the Haitian intellectuals would join our fellow peasants to save this knowledge that has proven vital in the past development of Haiti. *Kombitology* is an illustrative legacy of who we really are. We need to harness the power of collective action to achieve what we seek for ourselves. If our farmers can live with this practice so long and make it work, the Haitian elite can give it a new life in putting it on paper to be further developed. When we have all inculcated this way of life into our national identity, we will be able to roll back years of hardship that have plagued our dear nation.

One of the most effective weapons against poverty is education. When you educate a woman, you free her. It is time to start talking about what is important to us. It is time to start talking about education if we want to move from where we are to the next level. We are looking closely to see what new methods can be developed from the practice *kombitology*. People began to work together to solve existential problems. People were hungry. They needed food. To solve this problem, they joined their heads together to farm, plant and harvest. *Kombitology* has lessons for our politics. We must learn to solve problems as citizens of a nation, not as bickering partisans. Seeing how Haitian peasants used this practice to solve hunger problems, there is no excuse for us to sit and lament the lack of opportunities. Peasants are not sitting on their home sulking away. They are pitching themselves together against common problems. Peasants do not demonstrate on the street. They farm. Peasants do not compete. They harvest, produce to nourish us. We must be appreciative that they practice *kombitology,* in combination with other successful methods, to develop our country.

To live *kombitologically*, we must work together to produce goods for Haiti and for export. We must liberate ourselves through education so that we will be on the path of development. We must stop the street demonstrations and the needless competition. We should shun violence and make alliances. Let us learn how to solve our problems together. We should raise a new group of smart and intelligent leaders who like to help and take care of others. I hope we shall reach a state where everyone in Haiti is practicing *kombitocracy* in a new society where we are interconnected socially and are stronger economically.

KOMBITOCRACY

Piti piti, zwazo fè nich.
Little by little birds build their nests.
(Haitian Proverb)

Kombitocracy is a government of the people through the collective efforts of the people. It is not a one-party system that buoys development to an ideology or platform. Instead, it is a system that handles its problems through the people, instead of government. For instance, if a well is needed in Community A, the community will wait for government to release funding. In *kombitocracy*, the community goes ahead to build the well because it has resources to secure funding for the well. This approach cuts through the bureaucracy and places development in the hands of the various communities. Hence, the community that invests in itself gets the most projects.

We live in a democratic era. Therefore, we will make a small pull on the word *democracy* before I talk further about *kombitocracy*. One of the best definitions of democracy is from a great President of the United States (Abraham Lincoln) who defined democracy as 'the government of the people, by the people, for the people.'

In every society, you have two groups: those who govern and those who are governed. The people elect officials in elections to represent and to make decisions on their behalf. It is the responsibility of those who govern to guide people in the right path of development and prosperity. In democracy, people have a lot of power on the day of elections. After that, the people sit waiting for elected officials to achieve great promises they made during the electoral period. If the governing class proves their effectiveness, people can vote for them again. If they do not get good results, people can vote for others. In countries with adequate democratic structures like the U.S.A, it gets pretty elaborate. There is competition to see which party can run the nation better than other ones. But in poor countries like Haiti, people compete to stay in power longer to make money. We have no problems with matters of making money if made through honest means. We believe that, in poor countries today, we should inject a healthy dosage of *konbit* (working together) in the democratic system and give birth to a new political system called *Kombitocracy.*

We define *kombitocracy* as the government of the people focused on reaching solution by working together. *Kombitocracy* can be a new form of policy that can enable poor countries to stay on the path of development. Because it is not a system that has come to replace the democracy. However, deplorable conditions will not help us move democratically. Actions such as rioting and chaos will do nothing for us. *Kombitocracy* should be a system where people will not limit their participation only in electing government officials, but cooperate in implementing the goal of shared prosperity for the nation. This means that *kombitocracy* will strengthen the democratic system. It will aid in the achievement of economic and social success of poor countries.

In *kombitocracy*, the people ought to continue to work closely with the governing officials even after elections. There should be good relationships between people and their leadership. Communities must have social centers with systems of communication technology to enable people to stay in touch with leadership. Even when they cannot meet in person, they still can meet virtually. In *kombitocracy*, the governed and the governing should partner against problems in society. It is about solutions.

We should spend all our energy in working together to achieve dreams for ourselves and our country. There must be no sitting waiting for government to do anything for us. We must learn to congratulate our government for all it has done right and collaborate with them to find ways and means to do what must be done. The desire to work hard, to obey the laws and love our country should be our motivations. We should not encourage or participate in the creation of violence. We must not compete in the sense of individual interest. We must set timeline and deadline on projects we understand. The work is begging to be done. We must take the plough and mow the fields of opportunity that lie before us.

Ultimately, we think *kombitocracy* should be among poor countries a tool of development that enables them to get things done. *Kombitocracy* is an intellectual production based on an enlightened social solidarity where we impose to ourselves a model of the classic idea: *one for all and all for one*. Where each person is in solidarity with the rest of society, the rest of society must not fail her/him. One of the biggest lessons of solidarity that Haiti has is the solidarity in the Haitian army where all soldiers must win together or die together. We must seek success together or we will all perish without trying. There is no society without solidarity. Today, we should see solidarity as a contract to stimulate progress. Solidarity is not a bad word. It has gotten things done in communities worldwide where governments were not in a position to be of any help. We must remember that, in the eyes of foreigners, all Haitians look alike. This helps us to understand and accept that, if one Haitian is suffering, all Haitians are suffering. Accordingly, the new society we intend to invent is one for all and all for one. *Kombitocracy* will produce a series of social progressions conducive to economic takeoff in poor countries like Haiti.

HAITI

Sonje lapli ki leve mayi ou la.
Remember the rain that grew you your corn.
(Haitian Proverb)

Welcome to the island known to its natives as *Ayiti*, *Bohio*, or *Kiskeya*. Later on, when Christopher Columbus chanced on it, he gave it the name *La Isla Española* ("the Spanish Island").

This was shortened to *Hispaniola*. This was because the island was so beautiful and charming to the explorers. I choose to go into the distant past to evoke the glory of this nation that has been through crisis after crisis, thanks to a mixture of poor leadership and a floundering economy. We cannot let our present conditions drown out the illustrious history of our nation. It is essential to reconnect with our past successes, in order to forge a future ripe with prosperity.

Had it not been for active support provided by Haiti, the struggle for independence in the Americas (the United States included) will not have been successful. Our fathers were great men and women, who had the moral fortitude to assist the efforts of men such as Jose de San Martin, Don Francisco de Miranda, Manuel Dorrego and Simon Bolivar. Even Bolivar, in a moment of gratitude, called the then Haitian president, Alexander Petion, the 'Author of our Liberty.' It was Haiti, under the leadership of Petion that defeated the French, British and Spanish armies as those countries fought against freedom in their American colonies. Our ancestors founded the first country in the American continent to gain independence, practice democracy, respect human rights and eradicate slavery. Haiti was the lighthouse of liberation in the Americas, helping its neighbors with her resources to break the shackles of oppression. This inspiring narrative has been drowned in stories of misery and self-inflicted calamities. It is time for us to own the telling of our story (and history) to the world. We cannot trust foreigners to present Haiti without bias born out of misconceptions, distortions and downright lies. We must also develop the knack of determining who, among our helpers, are friends and who are not. We come from good stock and must take pride in what our forebears have done, even though geopolitics has not always worked in our favor. We cannot excuse our failures on the subterfuge of enemies or the apathy of friends. We must rise up from pits of pity and determine our destiny through a thorough dedication to progress. There has to be an intentional intolerance for mediocrity on every level. It must not be accepted in individuals, communities and country.

History gives us tomes of information from which we can analyze what worked and what did not. Our past has enough pain to push us out of our stupor. It is futile to ponder over past failures without being galvanized towards a better state of affairs. Haiti has had enough problems and we cannot exacerbate it with a lack of action. We must use history as a light to warn us of things that, when permitted, will sabotage our progress. Our present circumstances should make us uncomfortable enough to throw ourselves into the work that ensures a prosperous future. I say these things to remind the average Haitian that all is not lost. As long as we have breath, brains and bearing, we can regain the glory that was ours. When we position ourselves in the right direction, our leaders will have no other choice than to follow us there.

Haiti has more than the eyes can see. It is a small country with an illustrious history. It is blessed with cultural and natural wealth. There is a welcoming essence when one enters the country. We only need to start educating ourselves and the rest of our world about a new Haiti.

.

In few words, we may say that Haiti has placed itself among the awe-inspiring history of the world. Haitian history spreads through Africa,

Europe, North and South America. We, Haitian people, must give ourselves the best ways to communicate better with the African continent, we must present Haiti to the African nations for we are one of the first products Africa had offered worldwide: a free nation that abolished slavery and accorded equality to all of its citizens. Our ancestors fought to create the first independent Republic of blacks in the new world.

Thus, Haitian tourism industry, under the auspices of the Haitian government, must create a series of tours that are cheaper for Africans who want to come and visit Haiti, the mother of freedom in the new world.

In the reconstruction of Haiti, it would be possible for the Haitian and the Spanish governments (with Spanish and Haitian business interests) to invest in the reconstruction of Hispaniola in Mole Saint Nicolas. In the same vein, the Haitian and French governments, together with French and Haitian investors, can develop adequate economic relations to rehabilitate all former French historical sites. Haiti "la Perle des Antilles," (Pearl of islands) should be rebuilt so French tourists can come and refresh their memories.

Before our independence of Haiti in 1804, we were only a collective of warriors, soldiers and farmers. That was not enough to make us fit in the new fashion world economy. But the world cannot forget how we carried the flag for freedom in assisting many other people in achieving independence. Thus, I was pleased when I heard the Haitian prime minister (*Laurent Lamothe*) suggest that we work hand in hand with all Latin American countries like Venezuela, Colombia, Ecuador, Bolivia et cetera. We have to help people interested in following the paths that Latin American liberators (like Francisco de Miranda and Simon Bolivar) took to liberate them from the

Spanish crown. Haiti helped Miranda and Bolivar with several military expeditions from Cayes and Jacmel (Haiti) to overthrow *esclavagiste* settlers in Latin America. Today, we must continue this relationship of Latin America which started in the time of Dessalines and Petion (our founding fathers), in the early 1800s. Tourist attractions in Jacmel and Cayes will be steps in the right direction.

People say Haiti is the backyard of America. This is true. Our ancestors were companions in arms fighting against the British in the War of Independence. During the siege of Savannah, Georgia (U.S) on 9 October 1779, there were about one thousand Haitian soldiers in the ranks of the American army that fought against the English colonialists. Henry Christophe, the King of Haiti, took his baptism of fire with his war horse on American battle grounds. All Haitians and Americans are invited to visit the monument dedicated to the Haitian soldiers in Savannah, Georgia (U.S.) for their participation in the attainment of American independence in 1779. Presently, Haiti has the largest fortress in the Americas, the Citadelle la Ferriere in Cap Haitian (Haiti), which was built by one King Henry Christophe. He was only 14 years old when he fought alongside the Americans in 1779. Let us show some love to our common Heroes by visiting these two places. To see the pictures, go to www.wolove.org and click on *Visit Haiti*. It will be great for American and Haitian governments to work together to develop the tourism potential encapsulated in this exciting piece of history.

We should not lie to ourselves. It will not be easy to establish good relationship or good communication, with the ex-colonial countries. This will take a long time, effort and goodwill between us those countries. For nearly a century, those countries had kept us away from their colonies. They did not want us to contaminate their slaves with ideas of freedom. We must go further and look into the motives of this people to understand why they are trying to present Haiti in a terrible light while, at the same time, they seek to help us. We cannot say that they are wicked, but when they talk about Haiti they cannot say otherwise. For example, in a recent UN report on insecurity, Haiti was listed as one of the countries that had less insecurity in the Americas. (***Global Study on Homicide, 2011.***) Nothing is being said about the efforts of the current government in turning the nation in the right direction. Our journeys through two centuries have led us from the slave-master relationships to poor-rich relationships. If we want to change our lives in the best sense of the term is that we give ourselves ways that we might be involved in coming up with solutions to our existential problems. Most of our friends are already there waiting. But every time we decide to change our lives we realize that nothing will change without effort. For example, when you have abscess on your buttocks, a nurse can pop it for you but that nurse will never feel your pain and sensation. I work in a hospital where nearly all the sick people experience a kind of pain in the body and mind. I feel sorry for the patients and I try my best to help but I can never feel their pain at 100%. However, if someone tells me that he/she is hungry, I understand that more than 100% because I have experienced it before. I will stop suffering in my soul and heart I participate in solving problems of hunger. For growing up in Haiti, where most of us do not eat every day, I know what it means to have an empty belly go through and abdominal distress. Ever since I was younger, I had to make a difference in the life of my fellow human beings. I take each decision in life in terms of the change it can bring about in the lives of others.

As a consequence, *Wolove* is a chance I have to actualize my dreams for Haiti and, by extension, the world. I invite everyone who is going to work with me to consider the good of man in all they do. It is the best way to spend one's life. Today, we are engaging in a war to end hunger and poverty in Haiti. Let us work hard day and night or 24/7. Let us obey the law. Let us love our country as we love ourselves. We can make Haiti beautiful and prosperous again. Haiti can become a model of socio-economic success. A time is coming when other countries will choose Haiti as an example of peace, prosperity and progress. To make this change possible in Haiti, we all need to learn English. Because, like the tourism minister of Haiti, *Madame Stephanie Villedrouin said*, we believe that tourism is the future economic success or a base to change Haiti Cherie. So we send congratulations to everyone: Haitians and foreigners who are committed to Haiti's success.

HELP HAITI

Wòch nan dlo pa konn doulè wòch nan solèy.
Stones in water don't know the pain of stones in the sun.
(Haitian Proverb)

In the past centuries, when people were hungry for liberty, Haiti fed it to them in copious amounts. Haiti was behind the liberation of many countries like the United States (warfare in Savannah) and Latin American countries (help for Francisco de Miranda and Simon Bolivar). Nevertheless, Haitians are now hungry for food. Giving someone a fish is giving him/her food for a day. Showing someone how to fish is giving him/her food for life. Quotation # 2279 from Laura Moncur's Motivational Quotations:

"Give a man a fish and you feed him for a day. Teach a man to fish and you feed him for a lifetime."

After the earthquake of January 2010 that struck Haiti, many people on the ground have made and continue to make solidarity with Haiti in cash, food and clothes. Nevertheless, life in Haiti continues to degrade further. We believe it is time to galvanize Haitians to take their destiny into their own hands. It is a period to start thinking aid in the sense of sharing knowledge and culture. The Americans, who send you gifts or food, work very hard, in order to be capable being of assistance to you. Surely, we need to eat every day, but it is time we take knowledge and expertise from our good friends who want to help us. Please stop offering us money, food, or clothing. Share your knowledge and technologies used to create wealth in your countries so we can do better in a world. Haiti can live comfortably if it is given the tools to recalibrate the engines of her economy. I hope that my experiences can help you better understand what I am talking about.

I arrived in America for over 10 years. United States is a place where everyone has an equal chance to advance in life. It is especially possible when you choose to do what is good for yourself and for the country. This means, if you choose to do bad things, they will put you in prison. If you choose to do what is good in the society or the community where you live, they will assist you in attaining the progress you seek. For example, when I came here, things weren't easier because I could not speak English at all. Thus, I started working as a dishwasher, a job that paid very little. That's why, the Latinos always saying "mucho trabajo y poquito dinero (a lot of work but no money." When I decided to go to school to change my life, I was able to pay for an English course from my savings. However, learning English was not the only thing I wanted to do. I decided to learn a trade. I knew what I wanted to learn but tuition was too high. I could not afford it. I asked a colleague from work called Pashawn, 'what do I do to get help to pay for a career that I want to learn? And she said to me, 'you can ask for help from the college.' So Howard Community College paid 90% of my class with the money that government and Howard community people put together to help those who do not have enough income but would like to learn a trade to serve the community. I learned a valuable lesson. All I had to do was to take a baby step in the right direction. When I did that, everything I need to complete that track was made available to me. If an individual can do this and be successful, why can't a community do it? What can't a nation do it?

Since 2005, with the skills I learned, I have been living a normal life, earning acceptable wages. Accordingly, the truth is that the beloved America did not give me money, food or clothes when I was in need. Rather, it helped me through training to acquire skills for life. To help the poor effectively is not in helping him/her eat for a day, but in helping him/her find a skill that will ensure that he/she never goes hungry again. The spirit continues in the iFriendnett Organization and iFriendnett.org, which help others out through the study of English, customer service skills and how to create a small business. We can leave the world a better place than we found it.

I cannot conclude this book without recalling a conversation with a colleague who worked with me as a dishwasher when I first arrived in the U.S. I used to go to school shortly after completing my work schedule One day he asked me this question: where are you going? Why you are in a rush?' I said: 'I am going to school to learn English.' He answered me: 'Man, you do not need to go to school when I can teach you English.' I answered him: 'Thank you very much for your kindness but I must go to school to learn a trade and find a better job.' He continued dissuade me by saying: 'You do not need to learn anything because they will never give you a better job because you are black.' I brushed it aside and continued to school. Today the result is clear, that coworker still works at the same place while I have made small advances in the society. It is true that friend was an African-American and he may still continue to under value the power of education. Knowledge is a beloved treasure. Let us share it with everybody. A well-educated world brings prosperity to us all.

Haiti is at the cusp of an awakening into greatness. Instead of giving her loans, train her students. Instead of giving her handouts, give her tools to work out her destiny. Instead of pitying her, challenge her to be better. The people of Haiti need a push in the right direction. Give her the resources, knowledge and knowhow. Partner with her in her efforts towards development. Give her communities the support they need to reach the autonomy they need, in order to develop themselves. This is beyond politics. This is a nation willing to work for its future. Its people are willing to change the way they do things. Its communities are willing to do what it takes to succeed. This is what Wolove is about. A Haiti that works and works hard. A Haiti filled with law-abiding citizens. A Haiti where the love of country fills every heart. A Haiti ready to partner any willing country or group to bring lasting change. This is the story of change yearning to be realized. I invite you to become a part of this story as it takes shape before our very eyes.

SCREENING

Jan ou vini, se jan yo resevwa ou.
The way you come, is the way they will receive you.
(Haitian Proverb)

In the summer of 2013: we started Wolove Small Credit Solidarity in one city in Haiti, with the support with the local authorities and Wolove Haiti Association. The model was fashioned after what the people of France did after the World War II. Life was very hard for the French so their government had asked scholars to write small, inexpensive books with cheap papers so they could share their great ideas with anyone with the eagerness to learn. This was to rebuild a France where everyone could work together to end poverty. In response to the governmental request, there was a trickle of scholars who left the cities to go back to rural areas to create small business partnerships with the peasants. In the end, those efforts paid off and that what make France what it is today.

It would be phenomenal if each Haitian in diaspora would devote time, talent and treasure to Haiti. It is time for every Haitian and every intelligent person on this beautiful island to look in the mirror and ask himself/herself the following question: what I must do to help Haiti to become prosperous? This explains the rationale behind this book. We want to share our ideas with you. We do not intend to be any better than others. We only want to contribute our part in building a new Haiti where things can be wonderful for those who work hard, for those who obey the law and love their country.

Let us take a look at this matter from personal perspectives. We have been living in the U.S. where people work harder than any other place on earth. This is my home today. We have to call a pig a pig, as the saying in Haiti: "si yon moun pa gen yon aktyèlman New York, kafe ou koule ak ma (if you do not have a friend nor relative in New York to send you food or money, will you not survive?) All this is an idea emanating from a culture of dependency where many of us become an intermediary between people overseas who provide us food and a latrine hole where all the bodily-recycled food goes. So when this diaspora loses his job or dies, assistance dries up. That why many people cry twice when a relative in diaspora dies. We have to change or replace the old culture with a new culture of integration and innovation. My friend, begging or receiving everything for free, is bad for you. Using personal experiences, I realized that after ten years of helping siblings and friends to eat in Haiti, there was no marked change in their lives. However, for the past few months, things have begun to change since I started a new business experiment with two sisters and a cousin who was already running a small business. I have not been sending money for food to them since then. Rather, they have become thrivent in their businesses and are now in positions to take care of their needs themselves. Things are going very well. They borrow money from me and pay a little bit of interest. This has become a cycle of financial management where every time they pay up on a loan, they get qualified to get a higher amount.

For a small business to grow you must obtain credit from a bank. That is why we plan to expand this little experiment that we call: Wolove Small Credit Solidarity in several areas in Haiti, in collaboration with farmers, leaders, local and national authorities. Together we can continue to invent a new Haiti.

In the summer of 2014, we would like to introduce a new program: WOLOVE Rental Guest Rooms. It will be a program in which the peasants can host tourists in their homes. We will do everything to collaborate with stakeholders to bring more jobs to the selected areas.

Everyone agrees that Haiti has many natural and historical treasures. To attract tourists in this day and age, we must develop our sites to world class standards. Haiti has beautiful beaches, mountains and valleys. Haiti always invites tourists to come visit. But if tourists come pouring in on us, we do not have many places to offer them to stay. For example, our neighboring Dominican Republic has more than 60,000 hotel rooms whereas Haiti has around 3,000 hotel rooms. Surely, there are more hotels in construction in Haiti as we speak, but it will take time to finish building them. Therefore, it is possible today under the supervision of the ministry of tourism and local authorities to create some housing development with peasants for tourists. This would create many jobs in the nation. We are thinking of building Wolove Rental Guest Room as a project in an area of Haiti, with the assistance of local authorities and our U.S. friends.

Bringing tourists in the peasant's room means leading sustainable development in rural settings.

To complement this project, we are training the peasants in three areas: English, customer service and small business creation. To materialize this dream, we plan to begin the sequence and preparation for the first group of peasants who started with us in the summer of 2013. We started with a small credit program that we baptize: Wolove small credit solidarity with women who already own small businesses. Often in the advanced world, when someone has an idea, he keeps it secret until he can develop it or sell it. We are not keeping anything secret because our discovery is a token of our love for Haiti for all she has done for us. We are ready to share our ideas with anybody and, any person, group or association that may consult us. There is no place for laziness and procrastination. We all have to work together for the advancement and progress of the Haitian society. Thanks in advance for your suggestions after reading this book. We "Wolove" you very much.

When a baby is learning how to walk, he/she falls, gets up and continues until he/she figures it out. It is similar in the life of a country. It is true that Haiti's decline began in 1825 when it had to close schools and universities to repay 21 billion dollars that the government of France had termed as *independence's debt*. Haiti is still learning how to walk in various aspects of life. She is already strong in areas such as freedom. It was Haiti that was the inspiration behind the struggle for independence and the abolishment of slavery in the world. In the struggle for independence, she has camaraderie with nations and people who seek a better world. For example, a band of Polish soldiers left the camp of French soldiers in the ranges to help Haitians fight for independence because of their conscience and belief in liberty.

After the Haitian war of independence ended, the Polish soldiers chose to stay in Haiti in an area known as Kazal. Their settlement was done with the help of Emperor Dessalines. This is why we choose to ask for help for Haiti in getting international solidarity in its quest for development. We want to celebrate all the good things others have already done for us and to develop more opportunities for our people.

Simplicity gets a lot of things done. For the 5 years that we spent in development work in Haiti from 1997 to 2002, we practiced a philosophy which was very practical in that we chose to do simple things that you can see with your eyes and touch with your hands without spending much money. In conjunction with many other comrades like Father Franrtz Grandroit O.P, sister Dadou, Anax, Balanse etc., we brought change to the lives of a small group of people in Dofine, Haiti. We helped the peasants to build 15 small ponds to raise fish,

15 small forests to grow trees and helped them to bring water to the top of a mountain for the first time. Those were some of the best moments in my life. I hope you will choose to take good actions that will allow you to experience the sweet taste of change in communities that badly need it.

This is a dream that is possible. It is already set in motion. It is working in the selected communities that have embraced it. Join us in empowering the people of Haiti in the pursuit of their destiny. There is nothing that cannot be done if we decide to be one in purpose.

REFERENCES

1 - www.grameen-info.org/

2 - www.iFriendnett.org and IFriendnet Organization

3- www.wolove.org and Wolove Haiti Association

4- A little glances on social life in Haiti, America, France, Dominican Republic and Haiti.

5 - Method used: Investigation action

6 - A big thanks to the following:

Howard Community College
Hermione Gilet-Rigal
Judith A. Murray
Dorothy L. Moore
Bob Avel and his family
Jacob Lenji

ADDITIONAL RESOURCES

To learn more about how the idea of *Wolove* is changing communities in Haiti, visit www.wolove.org

To learn more about how the iFriendnet Organization is impacting students and professionals in Haiti and the Dominican Republic, visit www.ifriendnett.org

To book Bertony Paul for speaking engagements, visit www.bertonypaul.com.